Poems by the incomparable Mrs. K.P. (1664)

Katherine Philips

Poems by the incomparable Mrs. K.P.
Poems.
Philips, Katherine, 1631-1664.
Errata leaf inserted after p. 236.
[15], 242 p.
London : Printed by J.G. for Rich. Marriott ..., 1664.
Wing / P2032
English
Reproduction of the original in the Folger Shakespeare Library

Early English Books Online (EEBO) Editions

Imagine holding history in your hands.

Now you can. Digitally preserved and previously accessible only through libraries as Early English Books Online, this rare material is now available in single print editions. Thousands of books written between 1475 and 1700 and ranging from religion to astronomy, medicine to music, can be delivered to your doorstep in individual volumes of high-quality historical reproductions.

We have been compiling these historic treasures for more than 70 years. Long before such a thing as "digital" even existed, ProQuest founder Eugene Power began the noble task of preserving the British Museum's collection on microfilm. He then sought out other rare and endangered titles, providing unparalleled access to these works and collaborating with the world's top academic institutions to make them widely available for the first time. This project furthers that original vision.

These texts have now made the full journey -- from their original printing-press versions available only in rare-book rooms to online library access to new single volumes made possible by the partnership between artifact preservation and modern printing technology. A portion of the proceeds from every book sold supports the libraries and institutions that made this collection possible, and that still work to preserve these invaluable treasures passed down through time.

This is history, traveling through time since the dawn of printing to your own personal library.

Initial Proquest EEBO Print Editions collections include:

Early Literature

This comprehensive collection begins with the famous Elizabethan Era that saw such literary giants as Chaucer, Shakespeare and Marlowe, as well as the introduction of the sonnet. Traveling through Jacobean and Restoration literature, the highlight of this series is the Pollard and Redgrave 1475-1640 selection of the rarest works from the English Renaissance.

Early Documents of World History

This collection combines early English perspectives on world history with documentation of Parliament records, royal decrees and military documents that reveal the delicate balance of Church and State in early English government. For social historians, almanacs and calendars offer insight into daily life of common citizens. This exhaustively complete series presents a thorough picture of history through the English Civil War.

Historical Almanacs

Historically, almanacs served a variety of purposes from the more practical, such as planting and harvesting crops and plotting nautical routes, to predicting the future through the movements of the stars. This collection provides a wide range of consecutive years of "almanacks" and calendars that depict a vast array of everyday life as it was several hundred years ago.

Early History of Astronomy & Space

Humankind has studied the skies for centuries, seeking to find our place in the universe. Some of the most important discoveries in the field of astronomy were made in these texts recorded by ancient stargazers, but almost as impactful were the perspectives of those who considered their discoveries to be heresy. Any independent astronomer will find this an invaluable collection of titles arguing the truth of the cosmic system.

Early History of Industry & Science

Acting as a kind of historical Wall Street, this collection of industry manuals and records explores the thriving industries of construction; textile, especially wool and linen; salt; livestock; and many more.

Early English Wit, Poetry & Satire

The power of literary device was never more in its prime than during this period of history, where a wide array of political and religious satire mocked the status quo and poetry called humankind to transcend the rigors of daily life through love, God or principle. This series comments on historical patterns of the human condition that are still visible today.

Early English Drama & Theatre

This collection needs no introduction, combining the works of some of the greatest canonical writers of all time, including many plays composed for royalty such as Queen Elizabeth I and King Edward VI. In addition, this series includes history and criticism of drama, as well as examinations of technique.

Early History of Travel & Geography

Offering a fascinating view into the perception of the world during the sixteenth and seventeenth centuries, this collection includes accounts of Columbus's discovery of the Americas and encompasses most of the Age of Discovery, during which Europeans and their descendants intensively explored and mapped the world. This series is a wealth of information from some the most groundbreaking explorers.

Early Fables & Fairy Tales

This series includes many translations, some illustrated, of some of the most well-known mythologies of today, including Aesop's Fables and English fairy tales, as well as many Greek, Latin and even Oriental parables and criticism and interpretation on the subject.

Early Documents of Language & Linguistics

The evolution of English and foreign languages is documented in these original texts studying and recording early philology from the study of a variety of languages including Greek, Latin and Chinese, as well as multilingual volumes, to current slang and obscure words. Translations from Latin, Hebrew and Aramaic, grammar treatises and even dictionaries and guides to translation make this collection rich in cultures from around the world.

Early History of the Law

With extensive collections of land tenure and business law "forms" in Great Britain, this is a comprehensive resource for all kinds of early English legal precedents from feudal to constitutional law, Jewish and Jesuit law, laws about public finance to food supply and forestry, and even "immoral conditions." An abundance of law dictionaries, philosophy and history and criticism completes this series.

Early History of Kings, Queens and Royalty

This collection includes debates on the divine right of kings, royal statutes and proclamations, and political ballads and songs as related to a number of English kings and queens, with notable concentrations on foreign rulers King Louis IX and King Louis XIV of France, and King Philip II of Spain. Writings on ancient rulers and royal tradition focus on Scottish and Roman kings, Cleopatra and the Biblical kings Nebuchadnezzar and Solomon.

Early History of Love, Marriage & Sex

Human relationships intrigued and baffled thinkers and writers well before the postmodern age of psychology and self-help. Now readers can access the insights and intricacies of Anglo-Saxon interactions in sex and love, marriage and politics, and the truth that lies somewhere in between action and thought.

Early History of Medicine, Health & Disease

This series includes fascinating studies on the human brain from as early as the 16th century, as well as early studies on the physiological effects of tobacco use. Anatomy texts, medical treatises and wound treatment are also discussed, revealing the exponential development of medical theory and practice over more than two hundred years.

Early History of Logic, Science and Math

The "hard sciences" developed exponentially during the 16th and 17th centuries, both relying upon centuries of tradition and adding to the foundation of modern application, as is evidenced by this extensive collection. This is a rich collection of practical mathematics as applied to business, carpentry and geography as well as explorations of mathematical instruments and arithmetic; logic and logicians such as Aristotle and Socrates; and a number of scientific disciplines from natural history to physics.

Early History of Military, War and Weaponry

Any professional or amateur student of war will thrill at the untold riches in this collection of war theory and practice in the early Western World. The Age of Discovery and Enlightenment was also a time of great political and religious unrest, revealed in accounts of conflicts such as the Wars of the Roses.

Early History of Food

This collection combines the commercial aspects of food handling, preservation and supply to the more specific aspects of canning and preserving, meat carving, brewing beer and even candy-making with fruits and flowers, with a large resource of cookery and recipe books. Not to be forgotten is a "the great eater of Kent," a study in food habits.

Early History of Religion

From the beginning of recorded history we have looked to the heavens for inspiration and guidance. In these early religious documents, sermons, and pamphlets, we see the spiritual impact on the lives of both royalty and the commoner. We also get insights into a clergy that was growing ever more powerful as a political force. This is one of the world's largest collections of religious works of this type, revealing much about our interpretation of the modern church and spirituality.

Early Social Customs

Social customs, human interaction and leisure are the driving force of any culture. These unique and quirky works give us a glimpse of interesting aspects of day-to-day life as it existed in an earlier time. With books on games, sports, traditions, festivals, and hobbies it is one of the most fascinating collections in the series.

The BiblioLife Network

This project was made possible in part by the BiblioLife Network (BLN), a project aimed at addressing some of the huge challenges facing book preservationists around the world. The BLN includes libraries, library networks, archives, subject matter experts, online communities and library service providers. We believe every book ever published should be available as a high-quality print reproduction; printed on-demand anywhere in the world. This insures the ongoing accessibility of the content and helps generate sustainable revenue for the libraries and organizations that work to preserve these important materials.

The following book is in the "public domain" and represents an authentic reproduction of the text as printed by the original publisher. While we have attempted to accurately maintain the integrity of the original work, there are sometimes problems with the original work or the micro-film from which the books were digitized. This can result in minor errors in reproduction. Possible imperfections include missing and blurred pages, poor pictures, markings and other reproduction issues beyond our control. Because this work is culturally important, we have made it available as part of our commitment to protecting, preserving, and promoting the world's literature.

GUIDE TO FOLD-OUTS MAPS and OVERSIZED IMAGES

The book you are reading was digitized from microfilm captured over the past thirty to forty years. Years after the creation of the original microfilm, the book was converted to digital files and made available in an online database.

In an online database, page images do not need to conform to the size restrictions found in a printed book. When converting these images back into a printed bound book, the page sizes are standardized in ways that maintain the detail of the original. For large images, such as fold-out maps, the original page image is split into two or more pages

Guidelines used to determine how to split the page image follows:

• Some images are split vertically; large images require vertical and horizontal splits.
• For horizontal splits, the content is split left to right.
• For vertical splits, the content is split from top to bottom.
• For both vertical and horizontal splits, the image is processed from top left to bottom right.

Imprimatur.

Nov.25.1663.

Roger L'Estrange.

POEMS.

By the Incomparable, Mrs. K. P.

LONDON,

Printed by *J. G.* for *Rich. Marriott*, at his Shop under *S. Dunstans* Church in Fleet-street. 1664.

To the most excellently accomplish'd, Mrs. *K. P.* upon her Poems.

i.

WE allow'd your Beauty, and we did submit
    To all the tyrannies of it.
Ah, cruel Sex ! will you depose us too in Wit ?
    Orinda does in that too reign,
Does Man behind her in proud triumph draw,
And cancel great Apollo's Salick Law.
    We our old Title plead in vain :
Man may be Head, but Woman's now our Brain:
    Worse then Love's fire-arms heretofore :
    In Beauty's camp it was not known,
Too many arms, besides the Conquerour, bore.
    'Twas the great Cannon we brought down,
    T'assault the stubborn Town.
Orinda first did a bold sally make,
    Our strongest quarter take,

A 3   And

And so successful prov'd, that she
Turn'd upon Love himself his own Artillery.

2.

Women, as if the Body were the whole
Did that, and not the Soul,
Transmit to their posterity ;
If in it something they conceiv'd,
Th'abortive Issue never liv'd.
'Twere shame and pity, Orinda, if in thee
A Sp'rit so rich, so noble, and so high,
Should unmanur'd or barren lie.
But thou industriously hast sow'd and till'd
The fair and fruitful Field :
And 'tis a strange increase that it doth yield.
As when the happy Gods above
Meet all together at a Feast,
A secret joy unspeakably does move
In their great Mother Semele's contented breast :

With

With no less pleasure thou methinks should'st see
Thus thy no less immortal Progeny :
And in their Birth thou no one touch do'st find:
    Of th' ancient Curse to Woman-kind ;
        Thou bring' st not forth with pain,
It neither travel is nor labour of thy Brain.
    So easily they from thee come,
        And there is so much room
I'th' unexhausted and unfathom'd womb ;
That, like the Holland Countess, thou might' st bear
A Child for ev'ry day of all the fertile year.

                        3.

Thou dost my wonder, would' st my envy raise,
If to be prais'd I lov'd more then to praise.
    Where-e're I see an excellence,
I must admire to see thy well-knit Sense,
Thy Numbers gentle, and thy Passions high ;
                                        (Eye.
These as thy Forehead smooth, those sparkling as thy

            4 t.   'Tis

'Tis solid and 'tis manly all,

Or rather 'tis Angelical:

For, as in Angels, we

Do in thy Verses see

Both improv'd Sexes eminently meet;

They are then Man more strong, and more then Woman (sweet.

4.

They talk of Nine I know not who

Female Chimæra's that o're Poets reign;

I ne're could find that Fancy true,

But have invok'd them oft I'me sure in vain.

They talk of Sappho, but, alas! the shame

I'th' manners soil the lustre of her fame.

Orinda's inward Vertue is so bright,

That, like a Lantern's fair enclosed light,

It through the Paper shines where she doth write.

Honour and Friendship, and the gen'rous scorn

Of things for which we were not born,

(Things

(Things which of custom by a fond disease,
Like that of Girles, our vicious stomachs please)
Are the instructive subjects of her Pen.
    And as the Roman Victory
    Taught our rude Land arts and civility,
At once she takes, enslaves, and governs Men.

5.

But Rome with all her arts could ne're inspire
    A Female Breast with such a fire.
    The warlike Amazonian Train,
Which in Elysium now do peaceful reign,
And Wit's wild Empire before Arms prefer,
Find 'twill be settled in their Sex by her.
Merlin the Prophet (and sure he'l not lie
    In such an awful Company)
Does Prophecies of learn'd Orinda show,
What he had darkly spoke so long ago.

Even Boadicia's *angry Ghost*

Forgets her own misfortune and disgrace,

And to her injur'd Daughters now does boast,

That Rome's *o'recome at last by a Woman of her race.*

Abraham Cowley.

To the Incomparable Mrs. *K. P.* Author of these Poems.

Madam,

THe *Beauty of your Lines, is't not so clear*
    You need no Foil to make't the more appear ?
She that's Superlative, although alone
Consider'd, gains not by Comparison.
And yet whate're hath hitherto been writ
By others, tends to magnifie your Wit.
What's said of Origen, *(When he did well*
Interpret Texts, no man did him excell ;
When ill, no man did e're go so awry)
We may t'your Sex (though not to you) apply :
For now we've seen from a Feminine Quill
Poetry good as e're was, and as ill.

                                    H. A.

THE TABLE.

20

The Table.

The Table.

The Table.

POEMS.

POEMS.

I.

*Upon the double Murther of K. CHARLES I.
in Anfwer to a Libellous Copy of Rimes
made by Vavafor Powell.*

Think not on the State, nor am concern'd
Which way foever the great helm is turn'd:
But as that fon whofe father's dangers nigh
Did force his native dumbnefs, and untie
The fetter'd organs ; fo here's a fair caufe
That will excufe the breach of Nature's laws.
Silence were now a fin, nay Pafsion now
Wife men themfelves for Merit would allow.
What noble eye could fee (and carelefs pafs)
The dying Lion kick'd by every Afs ?

Has *Charles* so broke God's Laws, he must not have

A quiet Crown nor yet a quiet Grave?

Tombs have been Sanctuaries ; Thieves lie there

Secure from all their penalty and fear.

Great *Charles* his double misery was this,

Unfaithful Friends, ignoble Enemies.

Had any Heathen been this Prince's foe,

He would have wept to see him injur'd so.

His Title was his Crime, they'd reason good

To quarrel at the Right they had withstood.

He broke God's Laws, and therefore he must die ;

And what shall then become of thee and I ?

Slander must follow Treason ; but yet stay,

Take not our Reason with our King away.

Though you have seiz'd upon all our defence,

Yet do not sequester our common Sense.

But I admire not at this new supply :

No bounds will hold those who at **Sceptres** fly.

                                    Chri

Chrift will be King, but I ne're underftood
His Subjects built his Kingdom up with bloud,
Except their own; or that he would difpence
With his commands, though for his own defence.
Oh! to what height of horrour are they come
Who dare pull down a Crown, tear up a Tomb!

II.

On the numerous Accefs of the Englifh to wait upon the King in Flanders.

HAften, Great Prince, unto thy Britifh Ifles,
   Or all thy Subjects will become Exiles.
To thee they flock, thy Prefence is their home,
As *Pompey's* refidence made *Africk Rome.*
They that afferted thy Juft Caufe go hence
To teftifie their joy and reverence;
And thofe that did not, now, by wonder taught,
Go to confefs and expiate their fault.

So that if thou doſt ſtay, thy gaſping Land

Will it ſelf empty on the *Belgick* ſand :

Where the affrighted Dutchman does profeſs

He thinks it an Invaſion, not Addreſs.

As we unmonarch'd were for want of thee,

So till thou come we ſhall unpeopled be.

None but the cloſe Fanatick will remain,

Who by our Loyalty his ends will gain :

And he th'exhauſted Land will quickly find

As deſolate a place as he deſign'd.

For *England* (though grown old with woes) will ſee

Her long-deny'd and Soveraign Remedy.

So when old *Jacob* could but credit give

That his ſo long loſt *Joſeph* did ſtill live,

(*Joſeph* that was preſerved to reſtore

Their lives that would have taken his before)

It is enough, (ſaid he) *to Egypt I*

Will go, and ſee him once before I die.

III. Arion

III.
Arion *to a* Dolphin, *On His Majesty's* passage into England.

Whom does this stately Navy bring ?

O ! 'tis *Great Britain*'s Glorious King,

Convey him then, ye Winds and Seas,

Swift as Desire and calm as Peace.

In your Respect let him survey

What all his other Subjects pay ;

And prophesie to them again

The splendid smoothness of his Reign.

Charles and his mighty hopes you bear :

A greater now then *Cæsar* 's here ;

Whose Veins a richer Purple boast

Then ever Hero's yet engrost ;

Sprung from a Father so august,

He triumphs in his very dust.

In him two Miracles we view,

His Vertue and his Safety too :

For when compell'd by Traitors crimes

To breathe and bow in forein Climes,

Expos'd to all the rigid fate

That does on wither'd Greatnefs wait,

Had plots for Life and Confcience laid,

By Foes purfu'd, by Friends betray'd ;

Then Heaven, his fecret potent friend,

Did him from Drugs and Stabs defend ;

And, what 's more yet, kept him upright

'Midft flattering Hope and bloudy Fight.

Cromwell his whole Right never gain'd,

Defender of the Faith remain'd,

For which his Predeceffours fought

And writ, but none fo dearly bought.

Never was Prince fo much befieged,

At home provok'd, abroad obliged ;

Nor ever Man refifted thus,

No not great *Athanafius*.

No help of Friends could, or Foes fpight,

To fierce Invafion him invite.

Revenge to him no pleafure is,

He fpar'd their bloud who gap'd for his ;

Blufh'd any hands the Englifh Crown

Should faften on him but their own.

As Peace and Freedom with him went,

With him they came from Banifhment.

That he might his Dominions win,

He with himfelf did firft begin :

And that beft victory obtain'd,

His Kingdom quickly he regain'd.

Th' illuftrious fuff'rings of this Prince

Did all reduce and all convince.

He onely liv'd with fuch fuccefs,

That the whole world would fight with lefs.

Afsiftant Kings could but fubdue

Thofe Foes which he can pardon too.

He thinks no Slaughter-trophees good,

Nor Laurels dipt in Subjects blood ;

But with a fweet refiftlefs art

Difarms the hand, and wins the heart ;

And like a God doth refcue thofe

Who did themfelves and him oppofe.

Go, wondrous Prince, adorn that Throne

Which Birth and Merit make your own ;

And in your Mercy brighter fhine

Then in the Glories of your Line :

Find Love at home, and abroad Fear,

And Veneration every where.

Th' united world will you allow

Their Chief, to whom the *Englifh* bow :

And Monarchs fhall to yours refort,

As *Sheba's* Queen to *Judah's* Court ;

Returning

Returning thence conftrained more
To wonder, envy, and adore.
Difgufted *Rome* will hate your Crown,
But fhe fhall tremble at your Frown.

    For *England* fhall (rul'd and reftor'd by You)
    The fuppliant world protect, or elfe fubdue.

I V.
On the Fair Weather juft at Coronation.

So clear a feafon, and fo fnatch'd from ftorms,
    Shews Heav'n delights to fee what Man performs.
Well knew the Sun, if fuch a day were dim,
It would have been an injury to him:
For then a Cloud had from his eye conceal'd
The nobleft fight that ever he beheld.
He therefore check'd th' invading Rains we feared,
And a more bright *Parenthefis* appeared.

                  So

So that we knew not which look'd moft content,

The King, the People, or the Firmament.

But the Solemnity once fully paft,

* * * * * * * * *
* * * * * * * * *

And Heav'n and Earth each other to out-doe,

Vied both in Cannons and in Fire-works too.

So *Ifrael* paft through the divided floud,

While in obedient heaps the Ocean ftood :

But the fame Sea (the *Hebrews* once on fhore)

Return'd in torrents where it was before.

V.

To the *Queen's Majefty* on her *Arrival* at Portfmouth, May 14.1662.

NOw that the Seas & Winds fo kind are grown,

In our advantage to refign their own ;

Now you have quitted the triumphant Fleet,

And fuffered Englifh ground to kifs your Feet,

Whil'ft

Whil'ft your glad Subjects with impatience throng

To fee a Blefsing they have begg'd fo long ;

Whil'ft Nature (who in complement to you

Kept back till now her wealth and beauty too)

Hath, to attend the luftre your eyes bring,

Sent forth her lov'd Embaffadour the Spring ;

Whil'ft in your praife Fame's echo doth confpire

With the foft touches of the facred Lyre ;

Let an obfcurer Mufe upon her knees

Prefent you with fuch Offerings as thefe,

And you as a Divinity adore,

That fo your mercy may appear the more;

Who, though of thofe you fhould the beft receive,

Can fuch imperfect ones as thefe forgive.

Hail Royal Beauty, Virgin bright and great,

Who do our hopes fecure, our joyes complete.

We cannot reckon what to you we owe,

Who make Him happy who makes us be fo.

We

We did enjoy but half our King before,

You us our Prince and him his peace reſtore.

But Heav'n for us the deſp'rate debt hath paid,

Who ſuch a Monarch hath your Trophee made.

A Prince whoſe Vertue did alone ſubdue

Armies of Men, and of Offences too.

So good, that from him all our bleſſings flow,

Yet is a greater then he can beſtow.

So great, that he diſpences life and death,

And *Europe*'s fate depends upon his breath.

(For Fortune would her wrongs to him repair,

By Courtſhips greater then his Miſchiefs were:

As Lovers that of Jealouſie repent

Grow troubleſome in kind acknowledgment.)

Who greater courage ſhew'd in wooing you,

Then other Princes in their battels do.

Never was *Spain* ſo generouſly defi'd;

Where they deſign'd a Prey, he courts a Bride.

Hence

Hence they may guess what will his Anger prove,

When he appear'd so brave in making Love ;

And be more wise then to provoke his Arms,

Who can submit to nothing but your Charms.

And till they give him leisure to subdue,

His Enemies must owe their peace to you.

Whilest he and you mixing illustrious Rayes,

As much above our wishes as our praise,

Such Hero's shall produce, that even they

Without regret or blushes shall obey.

V I.
To the Queen-mother's Majesty,
Jan. 1. 166$\frac{0}{1}$.

YOu justly may forsake a Land which you

    Have found so guilty and so fatal too.

Fortune, injurious to your Innocence,

Shot all her poison'd arrows here, or hence.

                             'Twas

'Twas here bold Rebels once your Life pursu'd
(To whom 'twas Treason onely to be rude,)
Till you were forc'd by their unwearied spight
(O glorious Criminal !) to take your flight.
Whence after you all that was Humane fled ;
For here, oh ! here the Royal Martyr bled,
Whose cause and heart must be divine and high,
That having you could be content to die.
Here they purloin'd what we to you did owe,
And paid you in variety of woe.
Yet all those bellows in your breast did meet
A heart so firm, so loyal, and so sweet,
That over them you greater conquest made
Then your Immortal Father ever had.
For we may reade in story of some few
That fought like him, none that indur'd like you :
Till Sorrow blush'd to act what Traitors meant,
And Providence it self did first repent.

                                    But

But as our Active, so our Passive, ill

Hath made your share to be the sufferer's still.

As from our Mischiefs all your troubles grew,

'Tis your sad right to suffer for them too.

Else our Great *Charles* had not been hence so long,

Nor the Illustrious *Glou'ster* dy'd so young :

Nor had we lost a Princess all confest

To be the greatest, wisest, and the best ;

Who leaving colder parts, but less unkind,

(For it was here she set, and there she shin'd,)

Did to a most ungrateful Climate come

To make a Visit, and to find a Tomb.

So that we should as much your smile despair,

As of your stay in this unpurged air ;

But that your Mercy doth exceed our Crimes

As much as your Example former times,

And will forgive our Off'rings, though the flame

Does tremble still betwixt regret and shame.

For

For we have juftly fuffered more then you
By the fad guilt of all your fuff'rings too.
As you the great Idea have been feen
Of either fortune, and in both a Queen,
Live ftill triumphant by the nobleft wars,
And juftifie your reconciled ftars.
See your Offendors for your mercy bow,
And your tri'd Vertue all Mankind allow ;
While you to fuch a Race have given birth,
As are contended for by Heaven and Earth.

VII.
Upon the Princefs Royal her Return into England.

Welcome fure Pledge of reconciled Powers ;
   If Kingdoms have Good Angels, you are ours
For th' Ill ones check'd by your bright influence,
Could never ftrike till you were hurried hence.

S

But then, as Streams withstood more rapid grow;

War and Confusion soon did overflow :

Such and so many sorrows did succeed,

As it would be a new one now to reade.

But whil'st your Lustre was to us deny'd,

You scatter'd blessings every where beside.

Nature and Fortune have so gracious been,

To give you Worth, and Scene to shew it in.

But we do most admire that gen'rous Care

Which did your glorious Brother's sufferings share;

So that he thought them in your Presence none,

And yet your suff'rings did increase his own.

O wondrous prodigy! Oracle Divine!

Who owe more to your Actions then your Line.

Your Lives exalt your Father's deathless Name,

The blush of *England,* and the boast of Fame.

Pardon, Great Madam, this unfit Address,

Which does profane the Glory 'twould confess.

Our Crimes have banish'd us from you, and we

Were more remov'd by them then by the Sea.

Nor is it known whether we wrong'd you more

When we rebell'd, or now we do adore.

But what Guilt found, Devotion cannot miss;

And you who pardon'd that, will pardon this.

Your blest Return tells us our storms are ceased,

Our faults forgiven, and our stars appeased.

Your Mercy, which no Malice could destroy,

Shall first bestow, and then instruct, our Joy.

For bounteous Heav'n hath in your Highness sent

Our great Example, Bliss, and Ornament.

VIII.
On the Death of the Illustrious Duke of
Gloucester.

GReat *Glou'ster*'s dead, and yet in this we must
　　Confess that angry Heaven is wise and just.

We

We have ſo long and yet ſo ill endured
The woes which our offences had procured,
That this new ſtroke would all our ſtrength deſtroy,
Had we not known an intervall of Joy.
And yet perhaps this ſtroke had been excuſed,
If we this intervall had not abuſed.
But our Ingratitude and Diſcontent
Deſerv'd to know our mercies were but lent :
And thoſe complaints Heav'n in this rigid fate
Does firſt chaſtiſe, and then legitimate.
By this it our Diviſions does reprove,
And makes us joyn in grief, if not in love.
For (Glorious Youth) all Parties do agree,
As in admiring, ſo lamenting thee ;
The Soveraign Subject, Foreiners delight :
Thou wert the univerſal Favourite.
Not *Rome*'s belov'd and brave *Marcellus* fell
So much a Darling or a Miracle.

Built

Though built of richeft bloud and fineft earth,

Thou hadft a heart more noble then thy birth :

Which by th' afflictive changes thou didft know,

Thou hadft but too much caufe and time to fhew.

For when Fate did thy Infancy expofe

To the moft barbarous and ftupid Foes ;

Yet thou didft then fo much exprefs the Prince,

As did even them amaze, if not convince.

Nay, that loofe Tyrant whom no bound confin'd,

Who neither Laws nor Oaths nor Shame could bind,

Although his Soal was then his Look more grim,

Yet thy brave Innocence half foftened him.

And he that Worth wherein thy Soul was dreft

By his ill-favour'd clemency confeft ;

Leffening the ill which he could not repent,

He call'd that Travel which was Banifhment.

Efcap'd from him, thy Trials were encreas'd ;

The fcene was chang'd, but not the danger ceas'

Thou

Now from rough Guardians to Seducers gone,

Those made thy Temper, these thy Judgm.t known;

Whil'st thou the noblest Champion wert for Truth,

Whether we view thy Courage or thy Youth.

[...] to foil Nature and Ambition claims

Greater reward then to encounter Flames,

All that shall know the story must allow

[...] Martyr's Crown prepared for thy brow.

But yet thou wert suspended from thy Throne,

Til thy Great Brother had regain'd his own :

Who though the bravest Suff'rer, yet even he

Would not at once have mist his Crown and Thee.

But as Commission'd Angels make no stay,

But having done their errand go their way :

So thy part done, not thy restored State,

The future splendour which did for thee wait,

Nor that thy Prince and Countrey must mourn for

Such a Support and such a Counsellor,

Could longer keep thee from that blifs whence thou

Look'ft down with pity on Earth's Monarchs now ;

Where thy capacious Soul may quench her thirft,

And Younger Brother may inherit firft.

While on our King Heav'n does this care exprefs,

To make his Comforts fafe he makes them lefs.

For this fuccefsful Heathens ufe to fay,

It is too much, (*great Gods,*) *fend fome allay.*

IX.

To Her Royal Highnefs the Duchefs of York,
*on her commanding me to fend her fome
things that I had written.*

TO you whofe Dignity ftrikes us with aw,

   And whofe far greater Judgment gives us law,

Your Mind b'ing more tranfcendent then your State

For while but Knees to this, Hearts bow to that,

Thefe humble Papers never durft come near,

Had not your pow'rful Word bid them appear ;

In which such majesty, such sweetness dwells,

As in one act obliges and compells.

None can dispute commands vouchsaf'd by you.

What shall my fears then and confusion doe?

They must resign, and by their just pretence

Some value set on my obedience.

For in Religious Duties, 'tis confest,

The most Implicite are accepted best.

If on that score your Highness will excuse

This blushing tribute of an artless Muse,

She may (encourag'd by your least regard,

Which first did worth create, and then reward)

At modest distance with improved strains

That Mercy celebrate which now she gains.

But should you that severer justice use,

Which these too prompt Approches may produce,

As the swift Doe which hath escaped long,

Believes a Vulgar hand would be a wrong;

But

But wounded by a Prince falls without shame,

And what in life she loses, gains in fame :

So if a Ray from you chance to be sent,

Which to consume, and not to warm, is meant ;

My trembling Muse at least more nobly dies,

And falls by that a truer sacrifice.

X.
On the Death of the Queen of Bohemia.

ALthough the most do with officious heat

Onely adore the Living and the Great ;

Yet this Queen's Merits Fame hath so far spread,

That she rules still, though dispossest and dead.

For losing one, two other Crowns remain'd ;

Over all hearts and her own griefs she reign'd.

Two Thrones so splendid, as to none are less

But to that third which she does now possess.

Her

ler Heart and Birth Fortune fo well did know,

hat feeking her own fame in fuch a Foe,

he dreft the fpacious Theatre for the fight,

nd the admiring World call'd to the fight :

n Army then of mighty Sorrows brought,

Vho all againft this fingle Vertue fought ;

nd fometimes ftratagems, and fometimes blows

'o her Heroick Soul they did oppofe :

ut at her feet their vain attempts did fall,

nd fhe difcovered and fubdu'd them all.

ill Fortune weary of her malice grew,

ecame her Captive and her Trophee too :

nd by too late a fuit begg'd to have been

dmitted Subject to fo brave a Queen.

ut as fome Hero who a field hath wone,

Viewing the things he had fo bravely done,

Vhen by his fpirit's flight he finds that he

Vith his own Life muft buy the Victory,

He

He makes the slaughter'd heap that next him lies
His Funeral Pile, and then in triumph dies:
So fell this Royal Dame, with conquering spent,
And left in every breast her monument;
Wherein so high an Epitaph is writ,
As I must never dare to copy it.
But that bright Angel which did on her wait,
In fifty years contention with her fate,
And in that office did with wonder see
How great her troubles, how much greater she;
How she maintain'd her best Prerogative,
In keeping still the power to Forgive;
How high she did in her Directions go,
And how her Condescension stoop'd as low;
With how much Glory she had ever been
A Daughter, Sister, Mother, Wife, and Queen;
Will sure employ some deathless Muse to tell
Our children this instructive Miracle,

Wh

Who may her sad Illustrious Life recite,

And after all her Wrongs may doe her Right.

XI.
On the 3. of September, 1651.

AS when the glorious Magazine of Light

   Approches to his Canopy of Night,

He with new splendour clothes his dying Rayes,

And double brightnefs to his Beams conveys;

And, as to brave and check his ending fate,

Puts on his highest looks in 's lowest state,

Drest in such terrour as to make us all

Be *Anti-Perfians,* and adore his Fall;

Then quits the world, depriving it of Day,

While every Herb and Plant does droop away:

So when our gasping *English* Royalty

Perceiv'd her Period was now drawing nigh,

                      She

She fummons her whole ftrength to give one blow,

To raife her felf, or pull down others too.

Big with revenge and hope fhe now fpake more

Of terrour then in many moneths before ;

And mufters her Attendants, or to fave

Her from, or elfe attend her to, the Grave :

Yet but enjoy'd the miferable fate

Of fetting Majefty, to die in State.

Unhappy Kings, who cannot keep a Throne,

Nor be fo fortunate to fall alone !

Their weight finks others : *Pompey* could not fly,

But half the World muft bear him company ;

And captiv'd *Sampfon* could not life conclude,

Unlefs attended with a multitude.

Who 'd truft to Greatnefs now, whofe food is air,

Whofe ruine fudden, and whofe end defpair ?

Who would prefume upon his Glorious Birth,

Or quarrel for a fpacious fhare of Earth,

That

That fees fuch Diadems become fo cheap,

And Hero's tumble in a common heap :

Oh give me Vertue then, which fummes up all,

And firmly ftands when Crowns and Sceptres fall.

XII.

To the noble Palæmon, *on his incomparable*
Difcourfe of Friendfhip.

WE had been ftill undone, wrapt in difguife,

    Secure, not happy ; cunning, and not wife ;

War had been our defign, Intereft our trade ;

We had not dwelt in fafety, but in fhade,

Hadft thou not hung out Light more welcome far

Then wand'ring Sea-men think the Northern-ftar;

To fhew, left we our happinefs fhould mifs,

'Tis plac'd in Friendfhip, Mens and Angels blifs.

Friendfhip, which had a fcorn or mark been made,

And ftill had been derided or betray'd,

At

At which the great Physician still had laugh'd,

The Souldier stormed, and the Gallant scoff'd;

Or worn not as a Passion, but a Plot,

At first pretended, or at least forgot;

Hadst thou not been our great Deliverer,

At first discover'd, and then rescu'd her,

And raising what rude Malice had flung down,

Unveil'd her Face, and then restor'd her Crown:

By such august an action to convince,

'Tis greater to support then be a Prince.

Oh for a Voice which big as Thunder were,

That all Mankind thy conq'ring truths might hear!

Sure the Litigious as amaz'd would stand,

As Fairy Knights touch'd with *Cabina*'s Wand,

Drawn by thy softer, and yet stronger Charms,

* * * * * * * * * * *

And what more honour can on thee be hurl'd,

Then to protect a Vertue, save a World?

But while great Friendship thou haft copied out,

Thou 'ft drawn thy felf fo well, that we may doubt

Which moft appears, thy Candour or thy Art,

Or we owe more unto thy Brain or Heart.

But this we know without thine own confent,

Thou 'ft rais'd thy felf a glorious Monument ;

And that fo lafting that all Fate forbids,

And will out-live *Egyptian Pyramids.*

Temples and Statues Time will eat away,

And Tombs (like their Inhabitants) decay ;

But there *Palæmon* lives, and fo he muft

When Marbles crumble to forgotten duft.

XIII.
To the Right Honourable Alice Counteſs of
Carbury, on her enriching Wales with
her Preſence.

AS when the firft day dawn'd Man's greedy Eye

Was apt to dwell on the bright Prodigy,

Till

Till he might carelefs of his Organ grow,

And fo his wonder prove his danger too. :

So when your Countrey (which was deem'd to be

Clofe-mourner in its own obfcurity,

And in neglected Chaos fo long lay)

Was refcu'de by your beams into a Day,

Like men into a fudden luftre brought,

We juftly fear'd to gaze more then we ought.

2.

From hence it is you lofe moft of your Right,

Since none can pay 't, nor durft doe 't if they might

Perfection's mifery 'tis that Art and Wit,

While they would honour, do but injure it.

But as the Deity flights our Expence,

And loves Devotion more then Eloquence :

So 'tis our Confidence you are Divine,

Makes us at diftance thus approch your Shrine.

And

And thus fecur'd, to you who need no art,
I that fpeak leaft my wit may fpeak my heart.

3.

Then much above all zealous injury,
Receive this tribute of our fhades from me,
While your great Splendour, like eternal Spring,
To thefe fad Groves fuch a refrefhment bring,
That the defpifed Countrey may be grown,
And juftly too, the Envy of the Town.
That fo when all Mankind at length have loft
The Vertuous Grandeur which they once did boaft,
Of you like Pilgrims they may here obtain
Worth to recruit the dying world again.

D   XIV.

XIV.

To Sir Edw. Deering (*the noble* Silvander) *on his Dream and Navy, personating* Orinda's *preferring* Rosannia *before* Solomon's *Traffick to* Ophir.

THen am I happier then is the King ;

  My Merchandise does no such danger bring :

The Fleet I traffick with fears no such harms,

Sails in my sight, and anchors in my arms.

  Each new and unperceived grace

  Discovered in that mind and face,

  Each motion, smile and look from thee

  Brings pearls and *Ophir*-gold to me.

Thus far Sir Edw. Deering.

SIR, To be Noble when 'twas voted down,

To dare be Good though a whole Age should frown;

To live within, and from that even state

See all the under-world stoops to its fate ;

To

To give the Law of Honour, and difpence
All that is handfom, great and worthy thence ;
Are things at once your practice and your end,
And which I dare admire, but not commend.
But fince t' oblige the World is your delight,
You muft defcend within our watch and fight :
For fo Divinity muft take difguife,
Left Mortals perifh with the bright furprife.
And thus your Mufe, which can enough reward
All actions, ftudied to be brave and hard,
And Honours gives then Kings more permanent,
Above the reach of Acts of Parliament,
May fuffer an Acknowledgment from me,
For having thence receiv d Eternity.
My thoughts with fuch advantage you exprefs,
I hardly know them in this charming drefs.
And had I more unkindnefs for my friend
Then my demerits e're could apprehend,

Were

Were the Fleet courted with this gale of wind,

I might be sure a rich return to find.

So when the Shepherd of his Nymph complain'd,

Apollo in his shape his Mistress gain'd:

She might have scorn'd the Swain, & found excuse,

But could not this great Oratour refuse.

But for *Rosannia's* Interest I should fear

It would be hard t' obtain your pardon here.

But your first Goodness will, I know, allow

That what was Beauty then, is Mercy now.

Forgiveness is the noblest Charity,

And nothing can worthy your favour be.

For you (God-like) are so much your own fate,

That what you will accept you must create.

XV. T

X V.
To the truly-noble Mr. Henry Lawes.

NAture, which is the vaſt Creation's Soul,
   That ſteddy curious Agent in the whole,
The Art of Heaven, the Order of this Frame,
Is onely Number in another name.
For as ſome King conqu'ring what was his own,
Hath choice of ſeveral Titles to his Crown;
So Harmony on this ſcore now, that then,
Yet ſtill is all that takes and governs Men.
Beauty is but Compoſure, and we find
Content is but the Accord of the Mind,
Friendſhip the Union of well-tuned Hearts,
Honour 's the *Chorus* of the nobleſt parts,
And all the World on which we can reflect
Muſick to th' Ear, or to the Intellect.

If then each man a Little World muſt be,

How many Worlds are copied out in thee,

Who art ſo richly formed, ſo complete

T' epitomize all that is Good and Great;

Whoſe Stars this brave advantage did impart,

Thy Nature 's as harmonious as thy Art?

Thou doſt above the Poets praiſes live,

Who fetch from thee th' Eternity they give.

And as true Reaſon triumphs over Senſe,

Yet is ſubjected to Intelligence;

So Poets on the lower World look down,

But *Lawes* on them; his Height is all his own.

For, like Divinity it ſelf, his Lyre

Rewards the Wit it did at firſt inſpire,

And thus by double right Poets allow

His and their Laurel ſhould adorn his brow.

Live then, great Soul of Nature, to aſſwage

The ſavage dulneſs of this ſullen Age.

Charm

Charm us to Senfe ; for though Experience fail

And Reafon too, thy Numbers may prevail.

Then, like thofe Ancients, ftrike, and fo command

All Nature to obey thy gen'rous hand.

None will refift but fuch who needs will be

More ftupid then a Stone, a Fifh, a Tree.

Be it thy care our Age to new-create :

What built a World may fure repair a State.

XVI.

A Sea-voyage from Tenby *to* Briftoll, *begun*
Sept. 5. 1652. *fent from* Briftoll *to*
Lucafia *Sept.* 8. 1652.

Hoife up the fail, cri'd they who underftand

No word that carries kindnefs for the Land :

Such fons of clamour, that I wonder not

They love the Sea, whom fure fome Storm begot.

Had he who doubted Motion thefe men feen,

Or heard their tongues, he had convinced been.

For had our Bark mov'd half as faft as they,

We had not need caft anchor by the way.

One of the reft pretending to more wit,

Some fmall *Italian* fpoke, but murther'd it ;

For I (thanks :o *Saburna*'s Letters) knew

How to diftinguifh 'twixt the falfe and true.

But t' oppofe thefe as mad a thing would be

As 'tis to contradict a Presbyt'ry.

'Tis *Spanifh* though,(quoth I) e'en what you pleafe:

For him that fpoke it 'tmight be Bread andCheefe,

So foftly moves the Bark which none controuls,

As are the meetings of agreeing Souls :

And the Moon-beams did on the water play,

As if at Midnight 'twould create a Day.

The amorous Wave that fhar'd in fuch difpence

Expreft at once delight and reverence.

Such trepidation we in Lovers fpy

Under th' oppreffion of a Miftrefs eye.

Eut

But then the Wind so high did rise and roar,

Some vow'd they 'd never trust the traitor more.

Behold the fate that all our Glories sweep,

Writ in the dangerous wonders of the Deep :

And yet behold Man's easie folly more,

How soon we curse what erst we did adore.

Sure he that first himself did thus convey,

Had some strong passion that he would obey.

The Bark wrought hard, but found it was in vain

To make its party good against the Main,

Toss'd and retreated, till at last we see

She must be fast if e're she should be free.

We gravely Anchor cast, and patiently

Lie prisoners to the weather's cruelty.

We had nor Wind nor Tide, nor ought but Grief,

Till a kind Spring-tide was our first relief.

Then we float merrily, forgetting quite

The sad confinement of the stormy night.

E're

E're we had loft thefe thoughts, we ran aground,

And then how vain to be fecure, we found.

Now they were all furpriz'd. Well, if we muft,

Yet none fhall fay that duft is gone to duft.

But we are off now, and the civil Tide

Afsifted us the Tempefts to out-ride.

But what moft pleas'd my mind upon the way,

Was the Ship's pofture when 't in Harbour lay :

Which fo clofe to a rocky Grove was fixed,

That the Trees branches with the Tackling mixed.

One would have thought it was, as then it ftood,

A growing Navy, or a floating Wood.

But I have done at laft, and do confefs

My Voyage taught me fo much tedioufnefs.

In fhort, the Heav'ns muft needs propitious be,

Becaufe *Lucafia* was concern'd in me.

XVII. *Friend-*

XVII.

Friendship's Mystery, To my dearest Lucasia.
Set by Mr. Henry Lawes.

1.

COme, my *Lucasia*, since we see
    That Miracles Mens faith do move,
By wonders and by prodigy
    To the dull angry world let 's prove
    There 's a Religion in our Love.

2.

For though we were design'd t' agree,
    That Fate no liberty destroyes,
But our Election is as free
    As Angels, who with greedy choice
    Are yet determin'd to their joyes.

Our

3.

Our hearts are doubled by the lofs,
    Here Mixture is Addition grown ;
We both diffufe, and both ingrofs :
    And we whofe Minds are fo much one,
    Never, yet ever, are alone.

4.

We connt our own captinity.
    Then greateft thrones more innocent :
'Twere banifhment to be fet free,
    Since we wear fetters whofe intent
    Not Bondage is, but Ornament.

5.

Divided joyes are tedious found,
    And griefs united eafier grow :
We are our felves but by rebound,
    And all our Titles fhuffled fo,
    Both Princes and both Subjects too.

6.

Our Hearts are mutual Victims laid,
   While they (such power in Friendship lies)
Are Altars, Priests, and Off'rings made :
   And each Heart which thus kindly dies,
   Grows deathless by the Sacrifice.

XVIII.
Content, To my dearest Lucasia.

I.

COntent, the false World's best disguise,
   The search and faction of the Wife,
Is so abstruse and hid in night,
   That, like that Fairy Red-cross Knight,
Who trech'rous Falshood for clear Truth had got,
Men think they have it when they have it not.

For

2.

For Courts Content would gladly own,
But she ne're dwelt about a Throne:
And to be flatter'd, rich, and great,
Are things which do Mens senses cheat.
But grave Experience long since this did see,
Ambition and Content would ne're agree.

3.

Some vainer would Content expect
From what their bright Out-sides reflect:
But sure Content is more Divine
Then to be digg'd from Rock or Mine:
And they that know her beauties will confess,
She needs no lustre from a glittering dress.

4.

In Mirth some place her, but she scorns
Th' assistance of such crackling thorns,

Nor

Nor owes her felf to fuch thin fprot,

That is fo fharp and yet fo fhort :

And Painters tell us, they the fame ftrokes place

To make a laughing and a weeping face.

5.

Others there are that place Content

In Liberty from Government :

But who his Pafsions do deprave,

Though free from fhackles is a flave.

ontent and Bondage differ onely then,

Vhen we are chain'd by Vices, not by Men.

6.

Some think the Camp Content does know,

And that fhe fits o'th' Victor's brow :

But in his Laurel there is feen

Often a Cyprefs-bow between.

Ior will Content herfelf in that place give,

Vhere Noife and Tumult and Deftruction live.

But

7.

But yet the moſt Diſcreet believe,

The Schools this Jewel do receive;

And thus far's true without diſpute,

Knowledge is ſtill the ſweeteſt fruit.

But whilſt men ſeek for Truth they loſe their Peace,

And who heaps Knowledge, Sorrow doth increaſe.

8.

But now ſome ſullen Hermite ſmiles,

And thinks he all the World beguiles,

And that his Cell and Diſh contain

What all mankind wiſh for in vain.

But yet his Pleaſure 's follow'd with a Groan,

For man was never born to be alone.

'8.

Content her ſelf beſt comprehends

Betwixt two ſouls, and they two friends,

Whoſe

Whose either joyes in both are fixed,

And multiply'd by being mixed :

Whose minds and interests are still the same ;

Their Griefs, when once imparted, lose their name.

10.

These far remov'd from all bold noise,

And (what is worse) all hollow joyes,

Who never had a mean design,

Whose flame is serious and divine,

And calm, and even, must contented be,

For they 've both Union and Society.

11.

Then, my *Lucasia*, we have

Whatever Love can give or crave ;

With scorn or pity can survey

The Trifles which the most betray ;

With innocence and perfect friendship fired,

y Vertue joyn'd, and by our Choice retired.

E   Whose

12.

Whose Mirrours are the crystal Brooks,

Or else each others Hearts and Looks;

Who cannot wish for other things

Then Privacy and Friendship brings :
                                   (one,

Whose thoughts and persons chang'd and mixt are

Enjoy Content, or else the World hath none.

XIX.

A Dialogue of Absence'twixt Lucasia *and*
Orinda. *Set by Mr.* Hen. Lawes.

Luc. SAy, my *Orinda*, why so sad ?

    Orin. Absence frō thee doth tear my heart ;

Which, since with thine it union had,

    Each parting splits. *Luc.* And can we part ?

Orin. Our Bodies must. Luc. But never we :

Our Souls, without the help of Sense,

By

By wayes more noble and more free

Can meet, and hold intelligence.

Orin. And yet thofe Souls, when firft they met,

Lookt out at windows through the Eyes.

Luc. But foon did fuch acquaintance get,

Not Fate nor Time can them furprize.

Orin. Abfence will rob us of that blifs

To which this Friendfhip title brings :

Love's fruits and joyes are made by this

Ufelefs as Crowns to captiv'd Kings.

Luc. Friendfhip 's a Science, and we know

There Contemplation 's moft employ'd.

Orin. Religion 's fo, but practick too,

And both by niceties deftroy'd.

Luc. But who ne're parts can never meet,

And fo that happinefs were loft.

Orin. Thus Pain and Death are fadly fweet,

Since Health and Heav'n fuch price muft coft.

E 2   *Chorus.*

POEMS.

Chorus.

But we shall come where no rude hand shall sever,
And there wee'l meet and part no more for ever.

XX.

To my dear Sister, Mrs. C. P. on her Nuptial.

WE will not like those men our offerings pay
  Who crown the cup, then think they crown
We make no garlands, nor an altar build,   (the day.
Which help not Joy, but Ostentation yield.
Where mirth is justly grounded these wild toyes

* * * * * * * * * *
  * * * * * * * * * *

2.

But these shall be my great Solemnities,
Orinda's wishes for Cassandra's bliss.
May her Content be as unmix'd and pure
As my Affection, and like that endure;

And

And that ſtrong Happineſs may ſhe ſtill find
Not owing to her Fortune, but her Mind.

3.

May her Content and Duty be the ſame,
And may ſhe know no Grief but in the name.
May his and her Pleaſure and Love be ſo
Involv'd and growing, that we may not know
Who moſt Affection or moſt Peace engroſt ;
Whoſe Love is ſtrongeſt, or whoſe Bliſs is moſt.

4.

May nothing accidental e're appear
But what ſhall with new bonds their Souls endear;
And may they count the hours as they paſs,
By their own Joys, and not by Sun or Glaſs :
While every day like this may ſacred prove
To Friendſhip, Gratitude, and ſtricteſt Love.

E 3   XXI.

XXI.
To Mr. Henry Vaughan, Silurist, *on his* Poems.

HAd I ador'd the multitude, and thence
    Got an antipathy to Wit and Sense,
And hugg'd that fate in hope the World would
                                              (grant
·Twas good affection to be ignorant;
Yet the least Ray of thy bright fancy seen,
I had converted, or excuseless been;
For each Birth of thy Muse to after-times
Shall expiate for all this Age's crimes.
First shines thy Amoret, twice crown'd by thee,
Once by thy Love, next by thy Poetry:
Where thou the best of Unions dost dispence,
Truth cloth'd in Wit, and Love in Innocence.
So that the muddiest Lovers may learn here,
No Fountains can be sweet that are not clear.

                                    There

here *Juvenal* reviv'd by thee declares

ow flat man's Joys are, and how mean his Cares;

nd generally upbraids the World that they

ould such a value for their Ruine pay.

t when thy sacred Muse diverts her Quill,

ie Landskip to design of *Leon*'s hill;

; nothing else was worthy her or thee,

we admire almost t' Idolatry.

hat Savage breast would not be rap'd to find

ch Jewels in such Cabinets enshrin'd ?

iou fill'd with Joys too great to see or count,

:fcend'ft from thence like *Moses* from the Mount,

id with a candid, yet unqueftion'd aw,

ftor'ft the Golden Age when Verse was Law,

tructing us, thou who fecur'ft thy fame,

iat nothing can difturb it but my name;

iy I have hopes that ftanding fo near thine

will lofe its drefs, and by degrees refine.

Li

Live till the difabufed World confent,

All Truths of Ufe, or Strength, or Ornament,

Are with fuch Harmony by thee difplay'd

As the whole World was firſt by Number made ;

   And from the charming Rigour thy Mufe brings,

   Learn, there's no pleafure but in ferious things.

XXII.
A retir'd Friendſhip, to Ardelia.

COme, my *Ardelia,* to this Bower,

   Where kindly mingling Souls awhile

Let's innocently ſpend an hour,

   And at all ferious follies ſmile.

2.

Here is no quarrelling for Crowns,

   Nor fear of changes in our Fate ;

No trembling at the great ones frowns,

   Nor any flavery of State.

          3.

Here's no difguife nor treachery,

   Nor any deep conceal'd defign;

From Bloud and Plots this place is free,

   And calm as are thofe looks of thine.

          4.

Here let us fit and blefs our Stars,

   Who did fuch happy quiet give,

As that remov'd from noife of Wars

   In one anothers hearts we live.

          5.

Why fhould we entertain a fear?

   Love cares not how the World is turn'd:

If crouds of dangers fhould appear,

   Yet Friendfhip can be unconcern'd.

                    We

6.

We wear about us such a charm,
   No horrour can be our offence;
For mischief's self can doe no harm
   To Friendship or to Innocence.

7.

Let's mark how soon Apollo's beams
   Command the flocks to quit their meat,
And not entreat the neighbouring Springs
   To quench their thirst, but cool their heat.

8.

In such a scorching Age as this
   Who would not ever seek a shade,
Deserve their Happiness to miss,
   As having their own peace betray'd.

9.

But we (of one anothers mind
   Assur'd) the boisterous World disdain;

                                    With

With quiet Souls and unconfin'd

Enjoy what Princes wifh in vain.

XXIII.

To Mrs. Mary Carne, *when* Philafter
courted her.

Madam,

AS fome great Conqueror who knows no bounds,

But hunting Honour in a thoufand wounds,

Purfues his rage, and thinks that Triumph cheap

That 's but attended with the common heap,

Till his more happy fortune doth afford

Some Royal Captive that deferv'd his fword,

And onely now is of his Laurel proud,

Thinking his dang'rous valour well beftow'd ;

But then retreats, and fpending hate no more,

Thinks Mercy now what Courage was before :

As

As Cowardise in fight, so equally
He doth abhor a bloudy Victory.
So, Madam, though your Beauty were allow'd
To be severe unto the yielding Croud,
That were subdu'd e're you an Object knew
Worthy your Conquest and your Mercy too;
Yet now 'tis gain'd, your Victory 's complete,
Onely your Clemency should be as great.
None will dispute the power of your Eyes,
That understands *Philaster* is their prize.
Hope not your Glory can have new access,
For all your future Trophees will grow less:
And with that Homage be you satisfi'd
From him that conquers all the World beside,
Nor let your Rigour now the Triumph blot,
And lose the honour which your Beauty got.
Be just and kind unto your Peace and Fame,
In being so to him, for they 're the same:

                                   And

And live and die at once, if you would be

Nobly tranfmitted to Pofterity.

Take heed left in thy ftory they perufe

A murther which no language can excufe :

But wifely fpare the trouble of one frown ;

Give him his happinefs, and know your own,

Thus fhall you be as Honour's felf efteem'd,

Who have one Sex oblig'd, your own redeem'd.

Thus the Religion due unto your Shrine

Shall be as Univerfal as Divine :

And that Devotion fhall this blefsing gain,

Which Law and Reafon do attempt in vain.

The World fhall joyn, maintaining but one ftrife,

Who fhall moft thank you for *Philafter's* life.

XXIV. the

XXIV.

To Mr. J. B. the noble Cratander, upon a
Composition of his which he was not willing
to own publickly.

AS when some injur'd Prince assumes Disguise,

   And strives to make his Carriage sympathize,

Yet hath a great becoming Meen and Air,

Which speaks him Royal spight of all his care :

So th' Issues of thy Soul can ne're be hid,

And the Sun's force may be as soon forbid

As thine obscur'd ; there is no shade so great

Through which it will not dart forth light and heat.

Thus we discover thee by thy own Day

Against thy will snatching the Cloud away.

Now the Piece shines, and though we will not say,

Parents can Souls, as Tapers lights, convey ;

Yet we must grant thy Soul transmitted here

In beams almost as lasting and as clear.

                                    And

And that's our highest praise, for that thy Mind
Thy Works could never a resemblance find.
That mind whose search can Nature's secret hand
At one great stroke discover and command,
Which cleareth times and things, before whose eyes
Nor Men nor Notions dare put on disguise.
And were all Authors now as much forgot
As prosperous Ignorance her self would plot,
Had we the rich supplies of thy own breast,
The knowing World would never miss the rest.
Men did before from Ignorance take their Fame,
But Learning's self is honour'd by thy Name.
Thou studiest not belief to introduce
Of Novelties, more fit for shew then use;
But think'st it noble Charity t' uphold
The credit and the Beauty of the old:
And with one hand canst easily support
Learning and Law, a Temple and a Court.

And

And this secures me: for as we below
Valleys from Hills, Houses from Churches know,
But to their fight who stand extremely high,
These forms will have one flat Equality:
So from a lower Soul I might well fear
A critick censure when survey'd too near;
But from *Cratander* (who above the best
Lives in a height which levells all the rest)
I may that Royalty of Soul expect,
That can at once both pardon and neglect.
Thus I approch, and wanting wit and sense,
Let Trepidation be my Reverence.

XXV.
Lucasia.

NOt to oblige *Lucasia* by my voice,
To boast my fate, or justifie my choice

Is this defign'd ; but pity does engage

My Pen to refcue the declining Age.

For fince 'tis grown in fafhion to be bad,

And to be vain or angry, proud or mad,

(While in their Vices onely Men agree)

Is thought the onely modern Gallantry ;

How would fome brave Examples check the crimes,

And both reproch, and yet reform, the Times ?

Nor can Mortality it felf reclaim

Th' apoftate World like my *Lucafia*'s name :

Lucafia, whofe rich Soul had it been known

In that Time th' Ancients call'd the *Golden* one,

When Innocence and Greatnefs were the fame,

And Men no battels knew but in a game,

Chufing what Nature, not what Art, prefers ;

Poets were Judges, Kings Philofophers ;

Even then from her the Wife would copies draw,

And fhe to th' infant World had giv'n a Law.

F

That

That Souls were made of Number could not be

An Obfervation, but a Prophecy.

It meant *Lucafia*, whofe harmonious ftate

The Spheres and Mufes faintly imitate.

But as then Mufick is beft underftood,

When every Chord 's examin'd and found good ;

So what in others Judgment is and Will,

In her is the fame even Reafon ftill.

And as fome Colour various feems, but yet

'Tis but our diff'rence in confidering it :

So fhe now light, and then does light difpence,

But is one fhining Orb of Excellence :

And that fo piercing when fhe Judgment takes,

She doth not fearch, but Intuition makes :

And her Difcoveries more eafie are

Then *Cæfar*'s Conqueft in his *Pontick* War.

As bright and vigorous her beams are pure,

And in their own rich candour fo fecure,

That

That had she liv'd where Legends were devifed,

Rome had been juft, and fhe been canonized.

Nay Innocence her felf lefs clear muft be,

If Innocence be any thing but fhe.

For Vertue 's fo congenial to her mind,

That Liquid things, or Friends, are lefs combin'd.

So that in her that Sage his wifh had feen,

And Vertue 's felf had perfonated been.

Now as diftilled Simples do agree,

And in th' Alembick lofe variety ;

So Vertue, though in pieces fcatter'd 'twas,

by her Mind made one rich ufeful mafs.

Nor doth Difcretion put Religion down,

Nor hafty Zele ufurp the Judgment's crown.

Wifdom and Friendfhip have one fingle Throne,

And make another Friendfhip of their own.

Each fev'ral piece darts fuch fierce pleafing rayes,

Poetick Lovers would but wrong in praife.

Allhath proportion, all hath comlinefs,

And her Humility alone excefs.

Her Modefty doth wrong a Worth fo great,

Which Calumny herfelf would noblier treat:

While true to Friendfhip and to Nature's truft,

To her own Merits onely fhe 's unjuft.

But as Divinity we beft declare

By founds as broken as our Notions are;

So to acknowledge fuch vaft Eminence,

Imperfect Wonder is our evidence.

No Pen *Lucafia*'s glories can relate,

But they admire beft who dare imitate.

XXVI.
Wifton Vault.

ANd why this Vault and Tomb? alike we muft
Put off Diftinction, and put on Duft.

Nor

Nor can the stateliest fabrick help to save

From the corruptions of a common Grave;

Nor for the Resurrection more prepare,

Then if the Dust were scatter'd into air.

What then? Th' ambition 's just, say some, that we

May thus perpetuate our Memory.

Ah false vain task of Art! ah poor weak Man!

Whose Monument does more then 's Merit can:

Who by his Friends best care and love 's abused,

And in his very Epitaph misused:

For did they not suspect his Name would fall,

There would not need an Epitaph at all.

But after death too I would be alive,

And shall, if my *Lucasia* do, survive.

I quit these pomps of Death, and am content,

Having her Heart to be my Monument:

Though ne'reStone to me, 'twil Stone for me prove,

By the peculiar miracles of Love.

There I'le Infcription have which no Tomb gives,

Not, *Here Orinda lies*, but, *Here fhe lives.*

XXVII.
Friendfhip in Embleme, or the Seal.
To my deareft Lucafia.

1.

THE Hearts thus intermixed fpeak
   A Love that no bold fhock can break :
For joyn'd and growing both in one,
Neither can be difturb'd alone.

2.

That means a mutual Knowledge too;
For what is 't either Heart can doe,
Which by its panting Centinel
It does not to the other tell ?

That

3.

That Friendſhip Hearts ſo much refines,
It nothing but it ſelf deſigns :
The Hearts are free from lower ends,
For each point to the other tends.

4.

They flame, 'tis true, and ſeveral wayes,
But ſtill thoſe Flames do ſo much raiſe,
That while to either they incline
They yet are noble and divine.

5.

From ſmoke or hurt thoſe Flames are free
From groſneſs or mortality :
The Heart (like *Moſes* Buſh preſumed)
Warm'd and enlightned, not conſumed.

F 4

6.

The Compaſſes that ſtand above
Expreſs this great immortal Love ;
For Friends, like them, can prove this true,
They are, and yet they are not, two.

7.

And in their poſture is expreſt
Friendſhip's exalted Intereſt :
Each follows where the other leans,
And what each does each other means.

8.

And as when one foot does ſtand faſt,
And t'other circles ſeeks to caſt,
The ſteddy part does regulate
And make the Wandrer's motion ſtraight :

9.

So Friends are onely two in this,

T'reclaim each other when they miſs ;

For whoſoe're will groſly fall,

Can never be a Friend at all.

10.

And as that uſeful Inſtrument

 or Even lines was ever meant ;

 o Friendſhip from good Angels ſprings,

 o teach the world Heroick things.

11.

As theſe are found out in deſign

 o rule and meaſure every Line ;

 o Friendſhip governs actions beſt,

 reſcribing unto all the reſt.

12.

And as in Nature nothing 's set
So juſt as Lines in Number met ;
So Compaſſes for theſe b'ing made,
Do Friendſhip's harmony perſuade.

13.

And like to them, ſo Friends may own
Extenſion, not Diviſion :
Their Points, like Bodies, ſeparate ;
But Head, like Souls, knows no ſuch fate.

14.

And as each part ſo well is knit,
That their Embraces ever fit :
So Friends are ſuch by deſtiny,
And no third can the place ſupply.

15.

There needs no Motto to the Seal :
But that we may the mind reveal
To the dull Eye, it was thought fit
That *Friendſhip* onely ſhould be writ.

16.

ut as there are Degrees of bliſs,
o there 's no Friendſhip meant by this,
ut ſuch as will tranſmit to Fame
ucaſia and *Orinda*'s name.

XXVIII.

Memory of T. P. *who died at* Acton *the* 24.
May 1660. *at* 12. *and* ½ *of Age.*

F I could ever write a laſting Verſe,
It ſhould be laid, dear heart, upon thy Herſe.

But

But Sorrow is no Mufe, and does confefs

That it leaft can what it would moft exprefs.

Yet that I may fome bounds to Grief allow,

I'le try if I can weep in Numbers now.

Ah beauteous Bloffom too untimely dead !

Whither ? ah whither is thy fweetnefs fled ?

Where are the charms that alwayes did arife

From the prevailing language of thy Eyes ?

Where is thy lovely air and lovely meene,

And all the wonders that in thee were feen ?

Alas ! in vain, in vain on thee I rave ;

There is no pity in the ftupid Grave.

But fo the Bankrupt, fitting on the brim

Of thofe fierce Billows which had ruin'd him,

Begs for his loft Eftate, and does complain

To the inexorable Flouds in vain.

As well we may enquire when Rofes die,

To what retirement their fweet Odours flie ;

Whither

Whither their Virtues and their Bluſhes haſte,

When the ſhort triumph of their life is paſt ;

Or call their periſhing Beauties back with tears,

As adde one moment to thy finiſh'd years.

No, thou art gone, and thy preſaging Mind

So thriftily thy early hours deſign'd,

That haſty Death was baffled in his Pride,

Since nothing of thee but thy Body dy'd.

Thy Soul was up betimes, and ſo concern'd

To graſp all Excellence that could be learn'd,

That finding nothing fill her thirſting here,

To the Spring-head ſhe went to quench it there ;

And ſo prepar'd, that being freed from ſin

ſhe quickly might become a Cherubin.

Thou wert all Soul, and through thy Eyes it ſhin'd;

Aſham'd and angry to be ſo confin'd,

It long'd to be uncag'd, and thither flown

Where it might know as clearly as 'twas known.

In these vast hopes we might thy change have found,

But that Heav'n blinds whom it decrees to wound.

For Parts so soon at so sublime a pitch,

A Judgment so mature, Fancy so rich,

Never appear unto unthankful Men,

But as a Vision to be hid again.

So glorious Scenes in Masques Spectators view

With the short pleasure of an hour or two ;

But that once past, the Ornaments are gone,

The Lights extinguish'd, and the Curtains drawn

Yet all these Gifts were thy less noble part,

Nor was thy Head so worthy as thy Heart;

Where the Divine Impression shin'd so clear,

As snatch'd thee hence, and yet endear'd thee here:

For what in thee did most command our love

Was both the cause and sign of thy remove.

Such fools are we, so fatally we choose :

For what we most would keep we soonest loose.

The humble greatnefs of thy Pious thought,

Sweetnefs unforc'd, and Bafhfulnefs untaught,

The native Candour of thine open breaft,

And all the Beams wherein thy Worth was dreft,

Thy Wit fo bright, fo piercing and immenfe,

Adorn'd with wife and lovely Innocence,

Might have foretold thou wert not fo complete,

But that our joy might be as fhort as great.

'Tis fo, and all our cares and hopes of thee

Fled like a vanifh'd Dream or wither'd Tree.

So the poor Swain beholds his ripened Corn

By fome rough Wind without a Sickle torn.

Never, ah ! never let fad Parents guefs

At once remove of future happinefs:

But reckon Children 'mong thofe pafsing joys

Which one hour gives, and the next hour deftroys,

Alas ! we were fecure of our content ;

But find too late that it was onely lent,

To

To be a Mirrour wherein we may fee

How frail we are, how fpotlefs we fhould be.

But if to thy bleft Soul my grief appears,

Forgive and pity thefe injurious tears :

Impute them to Affection's fad excefs,

Which will not yield to Nature's tendernefs,

Since 'twas through deareft ties and higheft truft

Continued from thy Cradle to thy Duft ;

And fo rewarded and confirm'd by thine,

That (wo is me !) I thought thee too much mine.

But I'le refign, and follow thee as faft

As my unhappy Minutes will make haft.

Till when the frefh remembrances of thee

Shall be my Emblems of Mortality.

For fuch a lofs as this (bright Soul !) is not

Ever to be repaired or forgot.

XXIX. *In*

X X I X.

In memory of that excellent perfon Mrs. Mary Lloyd of Bodifcift in Denbigh-fhire, who died Nov.13.1656. after fhe came thither from Pembroke-fhire.

I Cannot hold, for though to write were rude,
  Yet to be filent were Ingratitude,
And Folly too ; for if Pofterity
  hould never hear of fuch a one as thee,
And onely know this Age's brutifh fame,
They would think Vertue nothing but a Name,
And though far abler Pens muft her define,
Yet her Adoption hath engaged mine :
  nd I muft own where Merit fhines fo clear,
Tis hard to write, but harder to forbear.
  prung from an ancient and an honour'd Stem,
Vho lent her luftre, and fhe paid it them ;

So ftill in great and noble things appeared,

Who yet their Country lov'd, and yet they feared,

Match'd to another as good and great as they,

Who did their Country both oblige and fway.

Behold herfelf, who had without difpute

More then both Families could contribute.

What early Beauty Grief and Age had broke,

Her lovely Reliques and her Offspring fpoke.

She was by nature and her Parents care

A Woman long before moft others are.

But yet that antedated feafon fhe

Improv'd to Vertue, not to Liberty.

For fhe was ftill in either ftate of life

Meek as a Virgin, Prudent as a Wife,

And fhe well knew, although fo young and fair,

Juftly to mix Obedience and Care;

Whil'ft to her Children fhe did ftill appear

So wifely kind, fo tenderly fevere,

That

That they from her Rule and Example brought

A native Honour, which she stampt and taught;

Nor can a single Pen enough commend

So kind a Sister and so dear a Friend.

A Wisdom from above did her secure,

Which though 'twas peaceable, was ever pure.

And if well-order'd Commonwealths must be

Paterns for every private Family,

Her House, rul'd by her hand and by her eye,

Might be a Patern for a Monarchy.

Her noble Beauty was her prudent Care,

Who handsom freedom gave, yet regular.

Solomon's wisest Woman less could doe ;

She built her house, but this preserv'd hers too.

She was so pious when that she did die,

She scarce chang'd Place, I'm sure not Company.

Her Zele was primitive and practick too ;

She did believe, and pray, and reade, and doe.

So firm and equal Soul she had engroft,

Juft ev'n to thofe that difoblig'd her moft,

She loft all fenfe of wrong, glad to believe

That it was in her power to Forgive.

Her Alms I may admire, but not relate,

But her own *works fhall praife her in the gate.*

Her Life was checquer'd with afflictive years,

And even her Comfort feafon'd in her Tears.

Scarce for a Husband's lofs her eyes were dried,

And that lofs by her Children half fupplied,

When Heav'n was pleas'd not thefe dear Props t'af-
                                              (ford,

But tore moft off by ficknefs or by fword.

She, who in them could ftill their Father boaft,

Was a frefh Widow every Son fhe loft.

Litigious hands did her of Light deprive,

That after all 'twas Penance to furvive.

She ftill thefe Griefs had nobly undergone,

Which few fupport at all, but better none.

                                    Such

Such a submissive Greatness who can find?

A tender Heart with so resolv'd a Mind?

But she, though sensible, was still the same,

Of a refined Soul, untainted Fame,

Nor were her Vertues coursly set, for she

Out-did Example in Civility.

To bestow blessings; to oblige, relieve,

Was all for which she could endure to live.

She had a joy higher in doing good,

Then they to whom the benefit accru'd.

Though none of Honour had a quicker sense,

Never had Woman more of Complaisance;

Yet lost it not in empty forms, but still

Her Nature noble was, her Soul gentile.

And as in Youth she did attract (for she

The Verdure had without the Vanity)

So she in Age was milde and grave to all,

Was not morose, but was majestical.

This

Thus from all other Women she had skill

To draw their good, but nothing of their ill.

And since she knew the mad tumultuous World,

Saw Crowns revers'd, Temples to ruine hurl'd;

She in Retirement chose to shine and burn,

As ancient Lamps in some *Egyptian* Urn.

At last, when spent with sickness, grief and age,

Her Guardian Angel did her death presage:

(So that by strong impulse she chearfully

Dispensed blessings, and went home to die;

That so she might, when to that place removed,

Marry his Ashes whom she ever loved)

She dy'd, gain'd a reward, and paid a debt.

The Sun himself did never brighter set.

Happy were they that knew her and her end,

More happy they that did from her descend:

A double blessing they may hope to have,

One she convey'd to them, and one she gave.

All

All that are hers are therefore sure to be

Bleft by Inheritance and Legacy.

A Royal Birth had lefs advantage been,

'Tis more to die a Saint then live a Queen.

XXX.

To the truly-competent Judge of Honour, Lucafia, upon a fcandalous Libel made by J. Jones.

HOnour, which differs man frō man much more

Then Reafon differ'd him from Beafts before,

Suffers this common Fate of all things good,

By the blind World to be mifunderftood.

For as fome Heathens did their Gods confine,

While in a Bird or Beaft they made their fhrine;

Depos'd their Deities to Earth, and then

Offer'd them Rites that were too low for Men:

So thofe who moft to Honour facrifice,

Prefcribe to her a mean and weak difguife;

Imprison her to others false Applause,

And from Opinion do receive their Laws,

While that inconstant Idol they implore,

Which in one breath can murther and adore.

From hence it is that those who Honour court,

(And place her in a popular report)

Do prostitute themselves to sordid Fate,

And from their Being oft degenerate.

And thus their Tenents are too low and bad,

As if 'twere honourable to be mad :

Or that their Honour had concerned been

But to conceal, not to forbear, a sin.

But Honour is more great and more sublime,

Above the battery of Fate or Time.

We see in Beauty certain airs are found,

Which not one Grace can make, but all compound,

Honour's to th' Mind as Beauty to the Sense,

The fair result of mixed Excellence,

As

As many Diamonds together lie,

And dart one luftre to amaze the Eye:

So Honour is that bright Ætherial Ray

Which many Stars doth in one light difplay.

But as that Beauty were as truly fweet,

Were there no Tongue to praife, no Eye to fee't;

And 'tis the Privilege of a native Spark,

To fhed a conftant Splendour in the dark:

So Honour is its own Reward and End,

And fatisfi'd within, cannot defcend

To beg the fuffrage of a vulgar Tongue,

Which by commending Vertue doth it wrong,

It is the Charter of a noble Action,

That the performance giveth fatisfaction.

Other things are below't; for from a Clown

Would any Conqueror receive his Crown?

'Tis reftlefs Cowardice to be a drudge

To an uncertain and unworthy Judge,

So the *Cameleon*, who lives on air,

Is of all Creatures moſt inclin'd to fear.

But peaceable reflexions on the Mind

Will in a ſilent ſhade Contentment find.

Honour keeps Court at home, and doth not fear

To be condemn'd abroad, if quiet there.

While I have this retreat, 'tis not the noiſe

Of Slander, though believ'd, can wrong my Joyes.

There is advantage in't : for Gold uncoin'd

Had been unuſeful, nor with glory ſhin'd :

This ſtamp'd my Innocency in the Ore,

Which was as much, but not ſo bright, before.

Till an *Alembick* wakes and outward draws,

The ſtrength of Sweets lies ſleeping in their Cauſe :

So this gave me an opportunity

To feed upon my own Integrity.

And though their Judgment I muſt ſtill diſclaim,

Who can nor give nor take away a fame :

Yet

Yet I'le appeal unto the knowing few,

Who dare be juſt, and rip his heart to you.

XXXI.
To Antenor, on a Paper of mine which J. Jones threatens to publiſh to prejudice him.

Muſt then my Crimes become his Scandal too?
   Why, ſure the Devil hath not much to doe.

The weakneſs of the other Charge is clear,

When ſuch a trifle muſt bring up the Rear.

But this is mad deſign, for who before

Loſt his Repute upon anothers ſcore?

My Love and Life I muſt confeſs are thine,

But not my Errours, they are only mine.

And if my Faults muſt be for thine allow'd,

It will be hard to diſſipate the Cloud:

For *Eve's* Rebellion did not *Adam* blaſt,

Untill himſelf forbidden Fruit did taſte.

                      'Tis

'T is possible this Magazine of Hell

'(Whose name would turn a Virge into a spell,

Whose mischief is congenial to his life)

May yet enjoy an honourable Wife.

Nor let his ill be reckoned as her blame,

Nor yet my Follies blast *Antenor*'s name.

But if those lines a Punishment could call

Lasting and great as this dark Lanthorn's gall;

Alone I'd court the Torments with content,

To testifie that thou art Innocent.

So if my Ink through malice prov'd a stain,

My Bloud should justly wash it off again.

But since that Mint of slander could invent

To make so dull a Ryme his Instrument,

Let Verse revenge the quarrel. But he's worse

Then wishes, and below a Poet's curse;

And more then this Wit knows not how to give,

Let him be still himself, and let him live.

XXXII. *To*

XXXII.
To the truly Noble Mrs. Anne Owen, on my first Approches.

Madam,

AS in a Triumph Conquerors admit
Their meanest Captives to attend on it,
Who, though unworthy, have the power confest,
And justifi'd the yielding of the rest:
So when the busie World, in hope t'excuse
Their own surprize, your Conquest do peruse,
And find my name, they will be apt to say,
Your charms were blinded, or else thrown away.
There is no honour got in gaining me,
Who am a prize not worth your Victory.
But this will clear you, that 'tis general,
The worst applaud what is admir'd by all.

But

But I have Plots in't: for the way to be

Secure of fame to all Posterity,

Is to obtain the honour I pursue,

To tell the World I was subdu'd by you.

And since in you all wonders common are,

Your Votaries may in your Vertues share,

While you by noble Magick worth impart :

She that can Conquer, can reclaim a heart.

Of this Creation I shall not despair,

Since for your own sake it concerns your care.

For 'tis more honour that the world should know,

You made a noble Soul, then found it so.

XXXIII.
Rosannia *shadowed whilest* Mrs. Mary Awbrey.

IF any could my dear *Rosannia* hate,

They onely should her Character relate.

Trut

Truth shines so bright there, that an enemy

Would be a better Oratour then I.

Love stifles Language, and I must confess,

I had said more if I had loved less.

Yet the most critical who that Face see

Will ne're suspect a partiality.

Others by time and by degrees persuade,

But her first look doth every heart invade.

She hath a Face so eminently bright,

Would make a Lover of an Anchorite:

A Face whose conquest mixt with modesty

Are both completed in Divinity.

Not her least glance but sets them all on fire,

And checks them if they would too much aspire,

Such is the Magick of her Looks, the same

Beam doth both kindle and refine our flame.

f she doth smile, no Painter e're would take

Another Rule when he would merry make.

And

And to her splendour Heaven hath allow'd,

That not a posture can her Beauty cloud:

For if she frown, none but would phansie then

Justice descended here to punish Men.

Her common looks I know not how to call

Any one Grace, they are compos'd of all.

And if we Mortals could the doctrine reach,

Her Eyes have language, and her Looks do teach,

Such is her whole frame, Heaven does afford

Her not to be desir'd, but still ador'd.

But as in Palaces the outmost worst

Rooms entertain our wonder at the first ;

But once within the Presence-chamber door,

We do despise whate're we saw before :

So when you with her Mind acquaintance get,

You'l hardly think upon the Cabinet,

Her Soul, that Ray shot from the Deity,

Doth still preserve its native purity ;

Whic

Which Earth can neither threaten or allure,

Nor by falfe joyes defile it, or obfcure.

Such Innocence within her heart doth dwell,

Angels themfelves do onely parallel.

And fhould her whole Sex to diffembling fall,

Her own Integrity redeems them all,

Tranfparent, clear, and will no words admit,

And all Comparifons but flubber it.

More gently foft then is an Evening-fhower:

And in that fweetnefs there is coucht a Power,

Which fcorning pride, doth think it very hard

If Modefty fhould need fo mean a Guard.

Her Honour is protected by her Eyes,

As the old Flaming Sword kept Paradife.

Such Conftancy of temper, truth and law,

Guides all her actions, that the World may draw

From her own felf the noblest Precedent

Of the moft fafe, wife, vertuous Government.

H   She

She courts Retirement, is herself alone
Above a Theatre, and beyon'd a Throne.
So rich a Soul, none can say properly
She hath, but is each noble Quality.
And as the highest Element is clear
From all the Tempests which disturb the Air:
So she above the World and its rude noise
Within a Storm a quiet Calm enjoys.
She scorns the sullen trifles of the Time,
But things transcendent do her thoughts sublime.
Unlike those Gallants which take far less care
To have their Souls then make their Bodies fair;
Who (sick with too much leisure) time do pass
With these two books, Pride and a Looking-glass:
Plot to surprize Mens hearts, their pow'r to try,
And call that Love which is mere Vanity.
But she, although the greatest Murtherer,
(For ev'ry glance commits a Massacre)

Yet

Yet glories not that flaves her power confefs,

But wifhes that her Monarchy were lefs.

And if fhe love, it is not thrown away,

As many doe, onely to fpend the day;

But her's is ferious, and enough alone

To make all Love become Religion.

Yea to her Friendfhip fhe fo faithful is,

That 'tis her onely blot and prejudice:

For Envy's felf could never errour fee

Within that Soul, 'bating her love to me.

Now as I muft confefs the name of Friend

To her that all the World doth comprehend

Is a moft wild Ambition; fo for me

To draw her picture is flat Lunacy.

Oh! I muft think the reft; for who can write

Or into words confine what's Infinite?

XXXIV.
To the Queen of Inconstancy, Regina Collie *in* Antwerp.

1.

UNworthy, since thou haſt decreed
    Thy Love and Honour both ſhall bleed,
My Friendſhip could not chuſe to die
In better time or company.

2.

What thou haſt got by this Exchange
Thou wilt perceive, when the Revenge
Shall by thoſe treacheries be made,
For which our Faith thou haſt betray'd.

3.

When thy Idolaters ſhall be
True to themſelves, and falſe to thee,

Thou'lt

Thou'lt fee that in Heart-merchandife,
Value, not Number, makes the price.

4.

Live to that day my Innocence
Shall be my Friendfhip's juft defence:
For this is all the World can find,
While thou wert noble, I was kind.

5.

The defp'rate game that thou doft play
At private Ruines cannot ftay;
The horrid treachery of that Face
Will fure undo its native place.

6.

Then let the Frenchmen never fear
The victory while thou art there:
For if Sins will call Judgments down,
Thou haft enough to ftock the Town.

XXXV.

To the Excellent Mrs. Anne Owen, upon h
receiving the name of Lucasia, and Adoption
into our Society, Decemb.28.1651.

WE are complete, and Fate hath now
    No greater blessing to bestow ;
No, the dull World must now confess
We have all worth, all happiness.
Annals of State are trifles to our fame,
Now 'tis made sacred by *Lucasia's* name.

But as though through a Burning-glass
The Sun more vigorous doth pass,
    Yet still with general freedom shines ;
    For that contracts, but not confines :
So though by this her beams are fixed here,
Yet she diffuses glory every where.

Her

Her Mind is so entirely bright,
The splendour would but wound our sight,
And must to some disguise submit,
Or we could never worship it.
And we by this relation are allow'd
Lustre enough to be *Lucasia*'s Cloud.

Nations will own us now to be
A Temple of Divinity ;
And Pilgrims shall ten Ages hence
Approch our Tombs with reverence.
May then that time which did such bliss convey
Be kept by us perpetual Holy-day.

XXXVI.
To my Excellent *Lucasia, on our Friendship.*

I Did not live untill this time
    Crown'd my felicity,
When I could say without a crime,
    I am not thine, but Thee.

This Carcass breath'd, and walkt, and slept,
    So that the World believ'd
There was a Soul the Motions kept ;
    But they were all deceiv'd.

For as a Watch by art is wound
    To motion, such was mine:
But never had *Orinda* found
    A Soul till she found thine ;

Whic

Which now inspires, cures and supplies,
  And guides my darkned Breast :
For thou art all that I can prize,
  My Joy, my Life, my Rest.

No Bridegrooms nor Crown-conquerors mirth
  To mine compar'd can be :
They have but pieces of this Earth,
  I've all the World in thee.

Then let our Flame still light and shine,
  And no false fear controul,
As innocent as our Design,
  Immortal as our Soul.

XXXVII. Ro-

XXXVII.
Rosannia's *private Marriage.*

IT was a wise and kind design of Fate,
    That none should this day's glory celebrate :
For 'twere in vain to keep a time which is
Above the reach of all Solemnities.
The greatest Actions pass without a noise,
And Tumults but prophane diviner Joyes.
Silence with things transcendent nearest suits,
The greatest Emperours are serv'd by Mutes.
And as in ancient time the Deities
To their own Priests reveal'd no Mysteries
Untill they were from all the World retir'd,
And in some Cave made fit to be inspir'd.
So when *Rosannia* (who hath them out-vied,
And with more Justice might be Deified ;

Who

Who if she had their Rites and Altars, we

Should hardly think it were Idolatry)

Had found a breast that did deserve to be

Receptacle of her Divinity ;

It was not fit the gazing World should know

When she convey'd her self to him, or how.

An Eagle safely may behold the Sun,

When weak Eyes are with too much Light undone.

Now as in Oracles were understood,

Not the Priests only, but the common good :

o her great Soul would not imparted be,

ut in design of general Charity.

he now is more diffusive then before;

nd what men then admir'd, they now adore.

or this Exchange makes not her Power less,

ut only fitter for the World's Address.

say then that Mind (which if we will admit

he Universe one Soul, must sure be it)

Inform this All, (which, till she shin'd out, lay

As drousie men do in a cloudy day)

And Honour, Vertue, Reason so dispence,

That all may owe them to her influence :

And while this Age is thus employ'd, may she

Scatter new Blessings for Posterity.

I dare not any other wish prefer,

For only her bestowing adds to her.

And to a Soul so in her self complete

As would be wrong'd by any Epithete,

Whose splendour's fix'd unto her chosen Sphear,

And fill'd with Love and Satisfaction there,

What can increase the Triumph, but to see

The World her Convert and her History :

XXXVIII. In-

XXXVIII.
Injuria Amiciciæ.

L Ovely Apoſtate ! what was my offence ?

Or am I puniſh'd for Obedience ?

Muſt thy ſtrange Rigour find as ſtrange a time ?

The Act and Seaſon are an equal Crime.

Of what thy moſt ingenuous ſcorns could doe

Muſt I be Subject and Spectatour too ?

Or were the Sufferings and Sins too few

To be ſuſtain'd by me, perform'd by you ?

Unleſs (with *Nero*) your uncurb'd deſire

Be to ſurvey the *Rome* you ſet on fire.

While wounded for and by your Power, I

t once your Martyr and your Proſpect die.

his is my doom, and ſuch a ridling Fate

s all impoſsibles doth complicate,

For Obligation here is Injury,

Conftancy Crime, Friendfhip a Herefie.

And you appear fo much on Ruine bent,

Your own deftruction gives you now Content :

For our twinne-Spirits did fo long agree,

You muft undoe your felf to ruine me.

And, like fome Frantick Goddefs, you'r inclin'd ;

To raze the Temple where you are enfhrin'd

And, what's the Miracle of Cruelty,

Kill that which gave you Immortality.

While glorious Friendfhip, whence your Honour (fprings,

Lies gafping in the Croud of common things ;

And I'me fo odious, that for being kind

Doubled and ftudied Murthers are defign'd.

Thy fin's all Paradox, for fhould'ft thou be

Thy felf again, th' wouldft be fevere to me.

For thy Repentance coming now fo late,

Would only change, and not relieve thy Fate.

So dangerous is the confequence of ill,

Thy leaft of Crimes is to be cruel ftill.

For of thy Smiles I fhould yet more complain,

If I fhould live to be betray'd again.

Live then (fair Tyrant) in Security,

From both my Kindnefs and Revenge be free;

While I, who to the Swains had fung your Fame,

And taught each Echo to repeat your Name,

Will now my private Sorrow entertain,

To Rocks and Rivers, not to thee, complain.

And though before our Union cherifh'd me,

'Tis now my pleafure that we difagree.

For from my Pafsion your laft Rigour grew,

And you kill'd me 'caufe that I worfhipp'd you.

But my worft Vows fhall be your Happinefs,

And not to be difturb'd by my diftrefs.

And though it would my facred flames pollute,

To make my heart a fcorned proftitute;

Yet

Yet I'le adore the Author of my Death,
And kiſs your Hand that robs me of my breath.

XXXIX.
To Regina Collier, *on her Cruelty to* Philaſter.

TRiumphant Queen of ſcorn! how ill doth ſit
In all that Sweetneſs ſuch injurious Wit?
Unjuſt and Cruel! what can be your prize,
To make one heart a double Sacrifice?
Where ſuch ingenuous Rigour you do ſhew,
To break his Heart, you break his Image too;
And by a Tyranny that's ſtrange and new,
You Murther him becauſe he Worſhips you.
No Pride can raiſe you, or can make him ſtart,
Since Love and Honour do enrich his heart.
Be Wiſe and Good, left when Fate will be juſt,
She ſhould o'rethrow thoſe glories in the duſt,

Riſle

Rifle your Beauties, and you thus forlorn
Make a cheap Victim to another's scorn;
And in those Fetters which you do upbraid
Your self a wretched Captive may be made:
Redeem the poyson'd Age, let it be seen
There's no such freedom as to serve a Queen.
But you I see are lately Round-head grown,
And whom you vanquish you insult upon.

XL.
To Philaster, *on his Melancholy for* Regina.

Give over now thy tears, thou vain
    And double Murtherer;
For every minute of thy pain
    Wounds both thy self and her,
Then leave this dulness; for 'tis our belief,
Thy Queen must cure, or not deserve, thy Grief.

I   XLI. Phi-

XLI.
Philoclea's *parting*, Feb. 25. 1650.

KInder then a condemned Man's Reprieve
    Was your dear Company that bad me live,
When by *Rofannia*'s filence I had been
The wretchedft Martyr any Age hath feen.
But as when Traytors faint upon the Rack,
Tormentors ftrive to call their Spirits back;
Not out of kindnefs to preferve their breath,
But to increafe the Torments of their Death:
So was I raifed to this glorious height,
To make my fall the more unfortunate.
But this I know, none ever dy'd before
Upon a fadder or a nobler fcore.

XLII.

To Rofannia, *now Mrs. Mountague,*
being with her, Septemb. 25.
1652.

1.

AS men that are with Viſions grac'd
Muſt have all other thoughts diſplac'd,
And buy thoſe ſhort deſcents of Light
With loſs of Senſe ; or Spirit's flight :

2.

So ſince thou wert my happineſs,
I could not hope the rate was leſs ;
And thus the Viſion which I gain
Is ſhort t' enjoy, and hard t' attain.

3.

Ah then ! what a poor trifle's all
That thing which here we Pleaſure call,

Since

Since what our very Souls hath coft
Is hardly got and quickly loft :

4.

Yet is there Juftice in the fate ;
For fhould we dwell in bleft eftate,
Our Joyes thereby would fo inflame,
We fhould forget from whence we came

5.

If this fo fad a doom can quit
Me for the follies I commit ;
Let no eftrangement on thy part
Adde a new ruine to my heart.

6.

When on my felf I do reflect,
I can no fmile from thee expect :
But if thy Kindnefs hath no plea,
Some freedom grant for Charity.

POEMS.

7.

Else the just World must needs deny
Our Friendship an Eternity :
This Love will ne're that title hold ;
For thine's too hot, and mine's too cold.

8.

Divided Rivers lose their name ;
And so our too-unequal flame
Parted, will Passion be in me,
And an Indifference in thee.

9.

Thy Absence I could easier find,
Provided thou wert well and kind,
Then such a Presence as is this,
Made up of snatches of my bliss.

10.

So when the Earth long gasps for rain,
If she at last some few drops gain,

I 3

She is more parched then at firſt ;

That ſmall recruit increas'd the thirſt.

XLIII.
To my Lucaſia.

LEt dull Philoſophers inquire no more

   In Nature's womb, or Cauſes ſtrive t' explore,

By what ſtrange harmony and courſe of things

Each body to the whole a tribute brings ;

What ſecret unions ſecret Neighbourings make,

And of each other how they do partake.

Theſe are but low Experiments : but he

That Nature's harmony intire would ſee,

Muſt ſearch agreeing Souls, ſit down and view

How ſweet the mixture is, how full, how true ;

By what ſoft touches Spirits greet and kiſs,

And in each other can complete their bliſs.

                 A won-

A wonder so sublime, it will admit

No rude Spectator to contemplate it.

The Object will refine, and he that can

Friendship revere must be a Noble man.

How much above the common rate of things

Must they then be from whom this Union springs?

But what's all this to me, who live to be

Disprover of my own Morality?

And he that knew my unimproved Soul,

Would say I meant all Friendship to controul.

But Bodies move in time, and so must Minds;

And though th' attempt no easie progress finds,

Yet quit me not, lest I should desp'rate grow,

And to such Friendship adde some Patience now.

O may good Heav'n but so much Vertue lend,

To make me fit to be *Lucasia*'s Friend!

But I'le forsake my self, and seek a new

Self in her breast that's far more rich and true.

Thus the poor Bee unmark'd doth humme and fly, S

And droan'd with age would unregarded dy, H

Unless some curious Artist thither come B

Will bless the Insect with an Amber-tomb, I

Then glorious in its funeral the Bee S

Gets Eminence and gets Eternity.

XLIV.
On Controversies in Religion.

RE igion, which true Policy befriends,

    Defign'd by God to ferve Man's nobleft ends,

Is by that old Deceiver's fubtile play

Made the chief party in its own decay,

And meets that Eagle's deftiny, whofe breaft

Felt the fame fhaft which his own feathers dreft.

For that great Enemy of Souls perceiv'd,

The notion of a Deity was weav'd

So closely in Man's Soul; to ruine that,

He must at once the World depopulate.

But as those Tyrants who their Wills pursue,

If they expound old Laws, need make no new :

So he advantage takes of Nature's light,

And raises that to a bare useless height ;

Or while we seek for Truth, he in the Quest

Mixes a Passion, or an Interest,

To make us lose it ; that, I know not how,

'Tis not our Practice, but our Quarrel now.

And as in th' Moon's Eclipse some Pagans thought

Their barbarous Clamours her deliverance wrought:

So we suppose that Truth oppressed lies,

And needs a Rescue from our Enmities.

But 'tis Injustice, and the Mind's Disease,

To think of gaining Truth by losing Peace.

Knowledge and Love, if true, do still unite;

God's Love and Knowledge are both Infinite.

And

And though indeed Truth does delight to lie

At some Remoteness from a Common Eye;

Yet 'tis not in a Thunder or a Noise,

But in soft Whispers and the stiller Voice.

Why should we then Knowledge so rudely treat,

Making our weapon what was meant our meat?

'Tis Ignorance that makes us quarrel so;

The Soul that's dark will be contracted too.

Chimæra's make a noise, swelling and vain,

And soon resolve to their own smoak again.

But a true Light the spirit doth dilate,

And robs it of its proud and sullen state;

Makes Love admir'd because 'tis understood,

And makes us Wise because it makes us Good.

'Tis to a right Prospect of things that we

Owe our Uprightness and our Charity.

For who resists a beam when shining bright,

Is not a Sinner of a common height.

That

That ſtate's a forfeiture, and helps are ſpent,

Not more a Sin then 'tis a Puniſhment.

The Soul which ſees things in their Native frame,

Without Opinion's Mask or Cuſtom's name,

Cannot be clogg'd to Senſe, or count that high

Which hath its Eſtimation from a Lie.

Mean ſordid things, which by miſtake we prize,

And abſent covet, but enjoy'd deſpiſe.)

But ſcorning theſe hath robb'd them of their art,

Either to ſwell or to ſubdue the Heart;

And learn'd that generous frame to be above

The World in hopes, below it all in love:

Touch'd with Divine and Inward Life doth run,

Not reſting till it hath its Centre won;

Moves ſteadily untill it ſafe doth lie

I'th' Root of all its Inmortality;

And reſting here hath yet activity

To grow more like unto the Deiry;

Good

Good, Univerſal, Wiſe and Juſt as he,

(The ſame in kind, though diff'ring in degree)

Till at the laſt 'tis ſwallow'd up and grown

With God and with the whole Creation one ;

It ſelf, ſo ſmall a part, i' th' Whole is loſt,

And Generals have Particulars engroſt.

That dark contracted Perſonality,

Like Miſts before the Sun, will from it flie.

And then the Soul, one ſhining ſphear, at length

With trueLove's wiſdomfill'd and purged ſtrength,

Beholds her higheſt good with open face,

And like him all the World ſhe can embrace.

XLV.
To the *Honoured Lady*, E. C.

Madam,

I Do not write to you that men may know

How much I'm honour'd that I may doe ſo :

Nor

Nor hope (though I your rich Example give)
To write with more fuccefs then I can live,
To cure the Age ; nor think I can be juft,
Who onely dare to write becaufe I muft.
I'm full of you, and fomething muft exprefs,
To vent my wonder and your pow'r confefs.
Let me then breathe in Verfe, which though undue,
The beft would feem fo when it fhadows you.
Had I ne're heard of your Illuftrious Name,
Nor known the *Scotch* or *Englifh* Honour's fame ;
Yet if your glorious Frame did but appear,
I fould have foon made all your Grandeur there.
I fould have feen in each majeftick ray
That Greatnefs Anceftours could e're convey ;
And in the luftre of your Eyes alone,
How near you were allied to the Throne :
Which yet doth leffen you, who cannot need
Thofe bright advantages which you exceed.

For

For you are such, that your Descent from Kings

Receives more Honour from you then it brings :

As much above their Glories as our Toil.

A Court to you were but a handsom foil.

And if we name the Stock on which you grew,

'Tis rather to doe right to it then you :

For those that would your greatest splendour see,

Must reade your Soul more then your **Pedigree.**

For as the sacred Temple had without

Beauty to feed those eyes that gaz'd about,

And yet had riches, state and wonder more,

For those that stood within the shining door :

But in the Holy place they admit few,

Lustre receiv'd and Inspiration too :

So though your Glories in your Face be seen,

And so much bright Instruction in your Meen ;

You are not known but where you will impart

The treasures of your more illustrious Heart.

Religion all her odours sheds on you,

Who by obeying vindicate her too :

For that rich Beam of Heaven was almost

In nice Disputes and false Pretences lost ;

So doubly injur'd, she could scarce subsist

Betwixt the Hypocrite and Casuist ;

Till you by great Example did convince

Us of her nature and her residence ,

And chose to shew her face, and ease her grief,

Less by your Arguments then by your Life ;

Which, if it should be copied out, would be

A solid Body of Divinity.

Your Principle and Practice light would give

What we should doe, and what we should believe :

For the extensive Knowledge you profess,

You do acquire with more ease then confess.

And as by you Knowledge has thus obtain'd

To be refin'd, and then to be explain'd :

So

So in return she useful is to you,

In Practice and in Contemplation too.

For by the various succours she hath lent,

You act with Judgment, and think with Content.

Yet those vast Parts with such a Temper meet,

That you can lay them at Religion's feet.

Nor is it half so bold as it is true,

That Vertue is her self oblig'd to you :

For being drest by your seducing Charms,

She conquers more then did the *Roman* Arms.

We see in you how much that Malice ly'd

That stuck on Goodness any sullen Pride ;

And that the harshness some Professours wear

Falls to their own, and not Religion's share.

But your bright Sweetness if it but appear,

Reclaims the bad, and softens the austere.

Men talk'd of Honour too, but could not tell

What was the secret of that active spell.

Th

That beauteous Mantle they to divers lent,

Yet wonder'd what the mighty Nothing meant.

Some did confine her to a worthy Fame,

And some to Royal Parents gave her Name.

You having claim unto her either way,

By what a King could give, a World could pay,

Have a more living Honour in your breast,

Which justifies, and yet obscures the rest ;

A Principle from Fame and Pomp unty'd,

So truly high that it despises Pride ;

Buying good actions at the dearest rate,

Looks down on ill with as much scorn as hate;

Acts things so generous and bravely hard,

And in obliging finds so much Reward ;

So Self-denying great, so firmly just,

Apt to confer, strict to preserve a Trust ;

That all whose Honour would be justified,

Must by your standards have it stamp'd and tried.

K   But

But your Perfection heightens others Crimes,

And you reproch while you inform the Times.

Which fad advantage you will scarce believe;

Or if you muft, you do conceal and grieve.

You fcorn fo poor a foil as others ill,

And are Protectour to th' unhappy ftill ;

Yet are fo tender when you fee a fpot,

You blufh for thofe who for themfelves could not.

You are fo much above your Sex, that we

Believe your Life our greateft courtefie :

For Women boaft, they have you while you live

A Pattern and a Reprefentative.

And future Mothers who in Child-bed groan,

Shall wifh for Daughters knowing you are one.

The world hath Kings whofe Crowns are cemented

Or by the bloud they boaft, or that they fhed :

Yet thefe great Idols of the ftooping crew

Have neither Pleafure found nor Honour true.

The

They either fight or play, and Power court,

In trivial anger or in civil sport.

You, who a nobler Privilege enjoy,

(For you can save whom they can but destroy)

An Empire have where different mixtures kiss;

You'r grave, not sour, and kind, but not remiss,

Such sweetned Majesty, such humble State

Do love and Reverence at once create.

Pardon (dear Madam) these untaught Essayes,

I can admire more fitly then I praise.

Things so sublime are dimly understood,

And you are born so great, and are so good,

So much above the Honour of your Name,

And by neglect do so secure your Fame;

Whose Beautie's such as captivates the Wise,

Yet you only of all the World despise;

That have so vast a Knowledge so subdued,

Religion so adorn'd, and so pursued;

K 2

A

A Wit ſo ſtrong, that who would it define,

Will need one ten times more acute then mine ;

Yet rul'd ſo that its Vigour manag'd thus

Becomes at once graceful and generous ;

Whoſe Honour has ſo delicate a Senſe,

Who alwayes pardon, never give offence ;

Who needing nothing, yet to all are kind,

Who have ſo large a Heart, ſo rich a Mind ;

Whoſe Friendſhip ſtill's of the obliging ſide,

And yet ſo free from tyranny and Pride ;

Who do in love like *Jonathan* deſcend,

And ſtrip your ſelf to cloath your happy friend ;

Whoſe kindneſs and whoſe modeſty is ſuch,

T' expect ſo little and deſerve ſo much ;

Who have ſuch candid worth, ſuch dear concern,

Where we ſo much may love, and ſo much learn ;

Whoſe very wonder though it fills and ſhines,

It never to an ill exceſs declines ;

But all are found so sweetly opposite,
As are in *Titian*'s Pieces Shade and Light:
That he that would your great Description try,
Though he write well, would be as lost as I,
Who of injurious Zele convicted stand,
To draw you with so bold and bad a hand;
But that, like other Glories, I presume
You will enlighten where you might consume.

XLVI.
Parting with Lucasia, *Jan.* 13. 1657.
A Song.

1.

WEll, we will doe that rigid thing
Which makes Spectators think we part;
Though Absence hath for none a sting
But those who keep each others heart.

And

2.

And when our Senſe is diſpoſſeſt,

    Our labouring Souls will heave and pant,

And graſp for one anothers breaſt,

    Since they their Conveyances want,

3.

Nay, we have felt the tedious ſmart

    Of abſent Friendſhip, and do know

That when we die we can but part;

    And who knows what we ſhall doe now?

4.

Yet I muſt go : we will ſubmit,

    And ſo our own Diſpoſers be ;

For while we noblier ſuffer it,

    We triumph o're Neceſsity.

5.

By this we ſhall be truly great,

    If having other things o're come,

To make our victory complete

    We can be Conquerors at home,

6.

Nay then to meet we may conclude,

    And all Obstructions overthrow,

Since we our Passion have subdu'd,

    Which is the strongest thing I know.

X L V I I.

Against Pleasure. Set by Dr. Coleman.

1.

THere's no such thing as Pleasure,

    'Tis all a perfect Cheat,

Which does but shine and disappear,

    Whose Charm is but Deceit :

The empty bribe of yielding Souls,

Which first betrays, and then controuls.

2.

'Tis true, it looks at diſtance fair ;
   But if we do approch,
The fruit of *Sodom* will impair,
   And periſh at a touch :
It being then in phancy leſs,
And we expect more then poſſeſs.

3.

For by our Pleaſures we are cloy'd,
   And ſo Deſire is done ;
Or elſe, like Rivers, they make wide
   The Channel where they run :
And either way true bliſs deſtroys,
Making Us narrow, or our Joys.

4.

We covet Pleaſure eaſily,
   But it not ſo poſſeſs ;

For many things muſt make it be,

But one way makes it leſs.

Nay, were our ſtate as we could chuſe it,

'Twould be conſum'd for fear to loſe it,

5.

What art thou then, thou winged Air,

More ſwift then winged Fame ?

Whoſe next ſucceſſour is Deſpair,

And its attendant Shame.

Th' Experience-Prince then reaſon had,

Who ſaid of Pleaſure, *It is mad.*

XLVIII.
Out of Mr. More's Cop. Conf.

THrice happy he whoſe Name is writ above,

Who doeth good though gaining infamy,

Requiteth evil turns with hearty love,

And cares not what befalls him outwardly ;

Whoſe

Whofe worth is in himfelf, and onely blifs

In his pure Confcience, which doth nought amifs:

Who placeth pleafure in his purged Soul,

    And Vertuous Life his treafure does efteem ;

Who can his Pafsions mafter and controul,

    And that true Lordly Manlinefs doth deem :

Who from this World himfelf hath dearly quit,

Counts nought his own but what lives in his fp'rit.

So when his Spirit from this vain World fhall flit,

    It bears all with it whatfoe're was dear

Unto it felf, pafsing an eafie Fit ;

    As kindly Corn ripened comes out of th' Ear,

Carelefs of what all idle men will fay,

He takes his own and calmly goes his way.

                       Etern

Eternal Reafon, Glorious Majefty,

Compar'd to whom what can be faid to be?

Whofe Attributes are Thee, who art alone

Caufe of all various things, and yet but One;

Whofe Effence can no more be fearch'd by Man,

Then Heav'n thy Throne be grafped with a Span,

Yet if this great Creation was defign'd

To feveral ends fitted for every kind;

Sure Man (the World's Epitome) muft be

Form'd to the beft, that is, to ftudy thee.

And as our Dignity, 'tis Duty too,

Which is fumm'd up in this, to know and doo.

Thefe comely rowes of Creatures fpell thy Name,

Whereby we grope to find from whence they came,

By thy own Change of Caufes brought to think

There muft be one, then find that higheft Link.

Thus all created Excellence we fee

Is a refemblance faint and dark of thee.

Such

Such shadows are produc'd by the Moon-beams
Of Trees or Houses in the running streams.
Yet by Imprefsions born with us we find
How good, great, just thou art, how unconfin'd.
Here we are swallow'd up, and daily dwell
Safely adoring what we cannot tell.
All we know is, thou art supremely good,
And dost delight to be so understood.
A spicy Mountain on the Universe,
On which thy richest Odours do disperse.
But as the Sea to fill a Veffel heaves
More greedily then any Cask receives,
Besieging round to find some gap in it,
Which will a new Infusion admit :
So dost thou covet that thou mayst dispence
Upon the empty World thy Influence ;
Lov'st to disburse thy self in kindnefs : Thus
The King of Kings waits to be gracious.

On

On this account, O God, enlarge my heart

To entertain what thou wouldst fain impart.

Nor let that Soul, by several titles thine,

And most capacious form'd for things Divine,

(So nobly meant, that when it most doth miss,

'Tis in mistaken pantings after Bliss)

Degrade it self in sordid things delight,

Or by prophaner mixtures lose its right.

Oh! that with fixt unbroken thoughts it may

Admire the light which does obscure the day.

And since 'tis Angels work it hath to doe,

May its composure be like Angels too.

When shall these clogs of Sense and Fancy break,

That I may hear the God within me speak?

When with a silent and retired art

Shall I with all this empty hurry part?

To the Still Voice above, my Soul, advance;

My light and joy's plac'd in his Countenance.

By

By whose dispence my Soul to such frame brought,

May tame each trech'rous, fix each scat'ring thought;

With such distinctions all things here behold,

And so to separate each dross from gold,

That nothing my free Soul may satisfie,

But t' imitate, enjoy, and study thee.

XLIX.

To Mrs. M. A. upon Absence. Set by
Mr. Hen. Lawes.

I.

'Tis now since I began to die

    Four Moneths and more, yet gasping live;

Wrapp'd up in sorrow do I lie,

    Hoping, yet doubting, a Reprieve.

Adam from Paradise expell'd

Just such a wretched being held.

'Tis

2.

'Tis not thy Love I fear to lose,
That will in spight of absence hold;
But 'tis the benefit and use
Is lost as in imprison'd Gold:
Which, though the Sum be ne're so great,
Enriches nothing but conceit.

3.

What angry Star then governs me
That I must feel a double smart,
Prisoner to fate as well as thee;
Kept from thy face, link'd to thy heart:
Because my Love all love excells,
Must my Grief have no Parallels:

4.

Sapless and dead as Winter here
I now remain, and all I see

Copies

Copies of my wild ſtate appear,
　　But I am their Epitome.
Love me no more, for I am grown
Too dead and dull for thee to own.

L.
L'Amitie. *To Mrs.* Mary Awbrey.

SOul of my Soul, my joy, my crown, my Friend,
　　A name which all the reſt doth comprehend ;
How happy are we now, whoſe Souls are grown
By an incomparable mixture one :
Whoſe well-acquainted Minds are now as near
As Love, or Vows, or Friendſhip can endear ?
I have no thought but what's to thee reveal'd,
Nor thou deſire that is from me conceal'd.
Thy Heart locks up my Secrets richly ſet,
And my Breaſt is thy private Cabinet.

Thou

Thou shed'st no tear but what my moisture lent,
And if I sigh, it is thy breath is spent,
United thus, what Horrour can appear
Worthy our Sorrow, Anger, or our Fear?
Let the dull World alone to talk and fight,
And with their vast Ambitions Nature fright;
Let them despise so Innocent a flame,
While Envy, Pride and Faction play their game:
But we by Love sublim'd so high shall rise,
To pity Kings, and Conquerours despise;
Since we that Sacred Union have engrost
Which they and all the sullen World have lost.

LI.

In Memory of Mr. Cartwright.

STay, Prince of Phancie, stay, we are not fit
To welcome or admire thy Raptures yet:

L   Such

Such horrid Ignorance benights the Times,

That Wit and Honour are become our Crimes.

But when those happy Pow'rs which guard thy duft

To us and to thy Mem'ry shall be just ,

And by a flame from thy bleſt Genius lent

Reſcue us from our dull Impriſonment ,

Unſequeſter our Fancies, and create

A Worth that may upon thy Glories wait :

We then shall underſtand thee, and deſcry

The ſplendour of reſtored Poetry.

Till when let no bold hand profane thy ſhrine,

'Tis high Wit-Treaſon to debaſe thy coin.

LII.

Mr. Francis Finch, *the Excellent* Palæmon.

THis is confeſt Preſumption, for had I

    All that rich ſtock of Ingenuity

Whic

Which I could wish for this, yet would it be

Palæmon's blot, a pious Injury.

ut as no Votaries are scorn'd when they

he meanest Victim in Religion pay ;

lot that the Pow'r they worship needs a gume,

ut that they speak their thanks for all with some :

) though the most contemptible of all

hat do themselves *Palæmon's* Servants call ,

know that Zele is more then Sacrifice,

or God did not the Widow's Mite despise,)

d that *Palæmon* hath Divinity,

d Mercy in its highest property :

that doth such transcendent Merit own,

ust have imperfect Offerings or none.

's one rich Lustre which doth Rayes dispence,

Knowledge will when set in Innocence.

Learning did select his noble breast,

here (in her native Majesty) to rest ;

Free

Free from the Tyranny and Pride of Schools,
Who have confin'd her to Pedantick Rules;
And that gentiler Errour which doth take
Offence at Learning for her Habit's fake:
Palæmon hath redeem'd her, who may be
Efteem'd himfelf an Univerfity;
And yet fo much a Gentleman, that he
Needs not (though he enjoys) a Pedigree.
Sure he was built and fent to let us know
What man completed could both be and doe.
Freedom from Vice is in him Nature's part,
Without the help of Difcipline or Art.
He's his own Happinefs and his own Law,
Whereby he keeps Pafsion and Fate in awe.
Nor was this wrought in him by Time and Growt
His Genius had anticipated both.
– Had all men been *Palæmons*, Pride had ne're
– Taught one man Tyranny, the other Fear;

Amb

mbition had been full as Monſtrous then

s this ill World doth render Worthy men.

ad men his Spirit, they would ſoon forbear

roveling for dirt, and quarrelling for air.

Vere his harmonious Soul diffus'd in all,

Ve ſhould believe that men did never fall.

is *Palæmon*'s Soul that hath engroſt

h' ingenuous candour that the World hath loſt;

Vhoſe own Mind ſeats him quiet, ſafe and high,

bove the reach of Time or Deſtiny.

was he that reſcu'd gaſping Friendſhip when

he Bell toll'd for her Funeral with men:

was he that made Friends more then Lovers burn,

nd then made Love to ſacred Friendſhip turn:

was he turn'd Honour inward, ſet her free

om Titles and from Popularity.

ow fix'd to Vertue ſhe begs Praiſe of none,

it's Witneſs'd and Rewarded both at home.

And

And in his breaſt this Honour's ſo enſhrin'd,

As the old Law was in the Ark confin'd :

To which Poſterity ſhall all conſent,

And leſs diſpute then Acts of Parliament.

He's our Original, by whom we ſee

How much we fail, and what we ought to be.

But why do I to Copy him pretend ?

My Rymes but libel whom they would commend.

'Tis true ; but none can reach what's ſet too high :

And though I miſs, I've noble Company :

For the moſt happy language muſt confeſs,

It doth obſcure *Palæmon*, not expreſs.

LIII.
To Mrs. M. A. at parting.

I.

I Have examin'd and do find,
   Of all that favour me

There's none I grieve to leave behind
   But onely onely thee.
To part with thee I needs muſt die,
Could Parting ſeparate thee and I.

2.

But neither Chance nor Complement
   Did element our Love ;
'Twas ſacred Sympathy was lent
   Us from the Quire above.
That Friendſhip Fortune did create
Still fears a wound from Time or Fate.

3.

Our chang'd and mingled Souls are grown
   To ſuch acquaintance now,
That if each would aſſume their own,
   Alas ! we know not how.
We have each other ſo engroſt,
That each is in the Union loſt.

L 4

4.

And thus we can no Abfence know,
   Nor fhall we be confin'd ;
Our active Souls will daily go.
   To learn each others mind.
Nay, fhould we never meet to Senfe,
Our Souls would hold Intelligence.

5.

Infpired with a Flame Divine
   I fcorn to court a ftay ;
For from that noble Soul of thine
   I ne're can be away.
But I fhall weep when thou doft grieve ;
Nor can I die whil'ft thou doft live.

6.

By my own temper I fhall guefs
   At thy felicity;

nd onely like thy happiness

  Because it pleaseth thee.

ur hearts at any time will tell

  thou or I be sick or well.

7.

ll Honour sure I must pretend,

  All that is Good or Great ;

e that would be *Rosannia*'s Friend,

  Must be at least complete.

I have any bravery,

  is 'cause I have so much of thee.

8.

y Leiger Soul in me shall lie,

  And all thy thoughts reveal ;

en back again with mine shall flie,

  And thence to me shall steal.

us still to one another tend ;

ch is the sacred name of *Friend*.

9.

Thus our twin-souls in one shall grow,

And teach the World new Love,

Redeem the Age and Sex, and shew

A Flame Fate dares not move:

And courting Death to be our friend,

Our Lives together too shall end.

10.

A Dew shall dwell upon our Tomb

Of such a quality,

That fighting Armies thither come

Shall reconciled be.

We'l ask no Epitaph, but say

ORINDA and *ROSANNIA.*

LIV.
To my dearest Antenor, on his Parting.

THough it be juſt to grieve when I muſt part
With him that is the Guardian of my Heart ;
Yet by an happy change the loſs of mine
Is with advantage paid in having thine.
And I (by that dear Gueſt inſtructed) find
Abſence can doe no hurt to Souls combin'd.
As we were born to love, brought to agree
By the impreſsions of Divine Decree :
So when united nearer we became,
It did not weaken, but increaſe, our Flame.
Unlike to thoſe who diſtant joys admire,
But ſlight them when poſſeſt of their deſire.
Each of our Souls did in its temper fit,
And in the other's Mould ſo faſhion'd it,

That

That now our Inclinations both are grown,

Like to our Interefts and Perfons, one ;

And Souls whom fuch an Union fortifies,

Pafsion can ne're deftroy, nor Fate furprize.

Now as in Watches, though we do not know

When the Hand moves, we find it ftill doth go :

So I, by fecret Sympathy inclin'd,

Will abfent meet, and underftand thy mind ;

And thou at thy return fhalt find thy Heart

Still fafe, with all the love thou didft impart.

For though that treafure I have ne're deferv'd,

It fhall with ftrong Religion be preferv'd.

And befides this thou fhalt in me furvey

Thy felf reflected while thou art away.

For what fome forward Arts do undertake,

The Images of abfent Friends to make,

And reprefent their actions in a Glafs,

Friendfhip it felf can onely bring to pafs,

That

That Magick which both Fate and Time beguiles,

And in a moment runs a thoufand miles.

So in my Breaft thy Picture drawn fhall be,

My Guide, Life, Object, Friend and Deftiny :

And none fhal know, though they imploy their wit,

Which is the right *Antenor*, thou, or it.

LV.

Engraven on Mr. John Collier's *Tomb-ftone at* Bedlington.

HEre what remains of him doth lie,

   Who was the World's Epitome,

Religion's Darling, Merchants Glory,

Mens true Delight, and Vertue's Story;

Who, though a Prifoner to the Grave,

A glorious Freedom once fhall have :

Till when no Monument is fit,

But what's beyond our love and wit.

LVI. *on*

LVI.
On the little Regina Collier, on the same Tomb-stone.

VErtue's Bloffom, Beautie's Bud,

   The Pride of all that's fair and good ,

By Death's fierce hand was fnatched hence

In her ftate of Innocence :

Who by it this advantage gains,

Her wages got without her pains.

LVII.
Friendfhip.

LEt the dull brutifh World that know not Love

   Continue Hereticks, and difapprove

That noble Flame ; but the refined know

'Tis all the Heaven we have here below.

                             Nature

ature subsists by Love, and they do tie

ings to their Causes but by Sympathy.

ve chains the different Elements in one

eat Harmony, link'd to the Heav'nly Throne.

id as on Earth, so the blest Quire above

Saints and Angels are maintain'd by Love;

lat is their Business and Felicity,

id will be so to all Eternity.

lat is the Ocean, our Affections here

e but streams borrow'd from the Fountain there.

id 'tis the noblest Argument to prove

Beauteous mind, that it knows how to Love.

lose kind Impressions which Fate can't controul,

e Heaven's mintage on a worthy Soul.

or Love is all the Arts Epitome,

id is the Sum of all Divinity.

e's worse then Beast that cannot Love, and yet

is not bought for Money, Pains or Wit;

For

For no change or defign can Spirits move,

But the Eternal deftiny of Love :

And when two Souls are chang'd and mixed fo,

It is what they and none but they can doe.

This, this is Friendfhip, that abftracted flame

Which groveling Mortals know not how to name,

All Love is facred, and the Marriage-tie

Hath much of Honour and Divinity.

But Luft, Defign, or fome unworthy ends

May mingle there, which are defpis'd by Friends,

Pafsion hath violent extreams, and thus

All oppofitions are contiguous.

So when the end is ferv'd their Love will bate,

If Friendfhip make it not more fortunate :

Friendfhip, that Love's Elixir, that pure fire

Which burns the clearer 'caufe it burns the higher.

For Love, like earthly fires (which will decay

If the material fuel be away)

Is

Is with offensive smoke accompanied,

And by resistance only is supplied :

But Friendship, like the fiery Element,

With its own Heat and Nourishment content,

Where neither hurt, nor smoke, nor noise is made,

Scorns the afsistance of a forein aid.

Friendship (like Heraldry) is hereby known,

Richeft when plaineft, braveft when alone,

Calm as a Virgin, and more Innocent

Then sleeping Doves are, and as much content

As Saints in Visions ; quiet as the Night,

But clear and open as the Summer's light ;

United more then Spirits Faculties,

Higher in thoughts then are the Eagle's eyes ;

Free as firft Agents are, true Friends and kind,

As but their selves I can no likenefs find.

M   LVIII. *The*

LVIII.
The Enquiry.

1.

IF we no old Hiftorian's name
   Authentick will admit,
But think all faid of Friendfhip's fame
   But Poetry or Wit :
Yet what's rever'd by Minds fo pure
Muft be a bright Idea fure.

2.

But as our Immortality
   By inward fenfe we find,
Judging that if it could not be,
   It would not be defign'd :
So here how could fuch Copies fall,
If there were no Original ?

3.

ut if **Truth** be in ancient Song,
   Or Story we believe,
the infpir'd and greater **Throng**
   Have fcorned to deceive ;
here have been **Hearts** whofe **Friendfhip** gave
hem thoughts at once both foft and grave.

4.

mong that confecrated **Crew**
   Some more Seraphick fhade
nd me a favourable **Clew**
   Now mifts my eyes invade.
hy, having fill'd the **World** with fame,
ft you fo little of your flame ?

5.

hy is't fo difficult to fee
Two Bodies and one **Mind** ?

M 2   **And**

And why are those who else agree

 So difficultly kind ?

Hath Nature such fantastick art,

That she can vary every Heart ?

6.

Why are the bands of Friendship tied

 With so remiss a knot,

That by the most it is defied,

 And by the most forgot ?

Why do we step with so light sense

From Friendship to Indifference ?

7.

If Friendship Sympathy impart,

 Why this ill-shuffled game,

That Heart can never meet with Heart,

 Or Flame encounter Flame ?

What does this Cruelty create ?

Is 't the Intrigue of Love or Fate ?

8.

ad Friendfhip ne're been known to Men,

(The Ghoft at laft confeft)

he World had then a ftranger been

To all that Heav'n poffeft.

ut could it all be here acquir'd,

ot Heav'n it felf would be defir'd.

LIX.
To my Lucafia, *in defence of declared Friendfhip.*

1.

My *Lucafia*, let us fpeak our Love,

And think not that impertinent can be,

'hich to us both doth fuch affurance prove,

And whence we find how juftly we agree.

2.

efore we knew the treafures of our Love,

Our noble aims our joys did entertain ;

M 3

And

And shall enjoyment nothing then improve?
    'Twere best for us then to begin again.

3.

Now we have gain'd, we must not stop, and sleep
    Out all the rest of our mysterious reign :
It is as hard and glorious to keep
    A victory, as it is to obtain.

4.

Nay, to what end did we once barter Minds,
    Onely to know and to neglect the claim?
Or (like some Wantons) our Pride pleasure finds
    To throw away the thing at which we aim.

5.

If this be all our Friendship does design,
    We covet not enjoyment then, but power :
To our Opinion we our Bliss confine,
    And love to have, but not to smell, the flower.

                        Ah!

6.

h ! then let Mifers bury thus their Gold,

Who though they ftarve no farthing wil produce:

ut we lov'd to enjoy and to behold,

And fure we cannot fpend our ftock by ufe.

7.

hink not 'tis needlefs to repeat defires ;

The fervent Turtles alwayes court and bill,

nd yet their fpotlefs pafsion never tires,

But does increafe by repetition ftill.

8.

lthough we know we love, yet while our Soul

Is thus imprifoned by the Flefh we wear,

here's no way left that bondage to controul,

But to convey tranfactions through the Ear.

9.

ay, though we reade our pafsions in the Eye,

It will oblige and pleafe to tell them too:

Such

Such joys as these by motion multiply,

    Were 't but to find that our Souls told us true.

10.

Believe not then, that being now secure

    Of either's heart, we have no more to doe :

The Spheres themselves by motion do endure,

    And they move on by Circulation too.

11.

And as a River, when it once hath paid

    The tribute which it to the Ocean owes,

Stops not, but turns, and having curl'd and play'd

    On its own waves, the shore it overflows :

12.

So the Soul's motion does not end in bliss,

    But on her self she scatters and dilates,

And on the Object doubles still ; by this

    She finds new joys which that reflux creates.

But

13.

But then because it cannot all contain,
    It seeks a vent by telling the glad news,
First to the Heart which did its joys obtain,
    Then to the Heart which did those joys produce.

14.

When my Soul then doth such excursions make,
    Unless thy Soul delight to meet it too,
What satisfaction can it give or take,
    Thou being absent at the interview?

15.

'Tis not Distrust; for were that plea allow'd,
    Letters and Visits all would useless grow:
Love, whose expression then would be its cloud,
    And it would be refin'd to nothing so.

16.

If I distrust, 'tis my own worth for thee,
    'Tis my own fitness for a love like thine;

And

And therefore ftill new evidence would fee,

    T' affure my wonder that thou canft be mine.

17.

But as the Morning-Sun to drooping Flowers,

    As weary Travellers a Shade do find,

As to the parched Violet Evening-fhowers ;

    Such is from thee to me a Look that's kind.

18.

But when that Look is dreft in Words, 'tis like

    The myftick pow'r of Mufick's union ;

Which when the Finger doth one Viol ftrike,

    The other's ftring heaves to reflection.

19.

Be kind to me, and juft then to your love,

    To which we owe our free and dear Converfe ;

And let not tract of Time wear or remove

    It from the privilege of that Commerce.

                           Tyrants

20.

yrants do banish what they can't requite :
But let us never know such mean desires ;
ut to be grateful to that Love delight
Which all our joys and noble thoughts inspires.

L X.
La Grandeur d'esprit.

Chosen Privacy, a cheap Content,
And all the Peace a Friendship ever lent,
Rock which civil Nature made a Seat,
Willow that repels the mid-day heat,
he beauteous quiet of a Summer's day,
Brook which sobb'd aloud and ran away,
vited my Repose, and then conspir'd
entertain my Phancie that retir'd.
Lucian's Ferry-man aloft did view
e angry World, and then laugh'd at it too:

So

So all its sullen Follies seem to me

But as a too-well acted Tragedy.

One dangerous Ambition doth befool,

Another Envies to see that man Rule:

One makes his Love the Parent of his Rage,

For private Friendship publickly t' engage:

And some for Confcience, some for Honour die;

And some are merely kill'd they know not why.

More different then mens faces are their ends,

Whom yet one common Ruine can make Friends.

Death, Duft and Darkness they have only won,

And haftily unto their Periods run.

Death is a Leveller; Beauty and Kings

And Conquerours, and all those glorious things

Are tumbled to their Graves in one rude heap,

Like common duft, as common and as cheap.

At greater Changes who would wonder then,

Since Kingdoms have their Fates as well as men?

They

They muſt fall ſick and die ; nothing can be

In this World certain, but uncertainty.

Since Pow'r and Greatneſs are ſuch ſlippery things,

Who'd pity Cottages, or envy Kings ?

Now leaſt of all, when, weary of deceit,

The World no longer flatters with the Great.

Though ſuch Confuſions here below we find,

As Providence were wanton with Mankind :

Yet in this Chaos ſome things do ſend forth,

Like Jewels in the dark, a Native worth.

He that derives his high Nobility,

Not from the mention of a Pedigree ;

Who thinks it not his Praiſe that others know

His Anceſtors were gallant long agoe ;

Who ſcorns to boaſt the Glories of his bloud,

And thinks he can't be great that is not good ;

Who knows the World, and what we Pleaſure call,

Yet cannot ſell one Conſcience for them all ;

VVho

Who hates to hoard that Gold with an excuse

For which he can find out a nobler use ;

Who dares not keep that Life that he can spend,

To serve his God, his Country, and his Friend ;

Falshood and Flattery doth so much hate,

He would not buy ten Lives at such a rate ;

Whose Soul, then Diamonds more rich and clear,

Naked and open as his face doth wear ;

Who dares be good alone in such a time,

When Vertue's held and punish'd as a Crime ;

Who thinks dark crooked Plots a mean defence,

And is both safe and wise in Innocence ;

Who dares both fight and die, but dares not fear ;

Whose only doubt is, if his cause be clear ;

Whose Courage and his Justice equal worn,

Can dangers grapple, overcome and scorn,

Yet not insult upon a conquer'd foe,

But can forgive him and oblige him too ;

Whose

hofe Friendfhip is coagenial with his Soul,

ho where he gives a heart beftows it whole,

hofe other ties and Titles here do end,

r buried or completed in the Friend ;

ho ne're refumes the Soul he once did give,

hile his Friend's Company and Honour live ;

nd if his Friend's content could coft the price,

ould count himfelf a happy Sacrifice ;

hofe happy days no Pride infects, nor can

is other Titles make him flight the man ;

o dark Ambitious thoughts do cloud his brow,

or reftlefs cares when to be Great and how ;

ho fcorns to envy Truth where e're it be,

ut pities fuch a Golden Slavery;

ith no mean fawnings can the people court,

or wholly flight a popular report ,

hofe houfe no Orphan groans do fhake or blaft,

or any riot of help to ferve his tafte ;

VVho

Who from the top of his Profperities

Can take a fall, and yet without furprize;

Who with the fame auguft and even ftate

Can entertain the beft and worft of Fate;

Whofe fuffering's fweet, if Honour once adorn it;

Who flights Revenge, not that he fears, but fcorns

Whofe Happinefs in ev'ry Fortune lives, (it;

For that no Fortune either takes or gives;

Who no unhandfome wayes can bribe his Fate,

Nay, out of Prifon marches through the Gate;

Who lofing all his Titles and his Pelf,

Nay, all the World, can never lofe himfelf;

This Perfon fhines indeed, and he that can

Be Vertuous is the great Immortal man.

LXI. *A*

LXI.
A Country-life.

HOw Sacred and how Innocent
   A Country-life appears,
How free from Tumult, Difcontent,
   From Flattery or Fears!
This was the firft and happieft Life,
   When man enjoy'd himfelf;
Till Pride exchanged Peace for Strife,
   And Happinefs for Pelf.
'Twas here the Poets were infpir'd,
   And fang their Myfteries;
And while the liftning World admir'd,
   Mens Minds did civilize.
That Golden Age did entertain
   No Pafsion but of Love;

N

The

The thoughts of Ruling and of Gain
   Did ne're their Fancies move.

None then did envy Neighbour's wealth,
   Nor Plot to wrong his bed :

Happy in Friendſhip and in Health,
   'On Roots, not Beaſts, they fed.

They knew no Law nor Phyſick then,
   Nature was all their Wit.

And if there yet remain to men
   Content, ſure this is it.

What Bleſsings doth this World afford
   To tempt or bribe deſire ?

For Courtſhip is all Fire and Sword,
   Who would not then retire ?

Then welcome deareſt Solitude,
   My great Felicity ;

Though ſome are pleas'd to call thee rude,
   Thou art not ſo, but we.

                               Such

Such as do covet only reſt

    A Cottage will ſuffice :

Is it not brave to be poſſeſt

    Of Earth but to deſpiſe ?

Opinion is the rate of things,

    From hence our Peace doth flow ;

I have a better Fate then Kings,

    Becauſe I think it ſo.

When all the ſtormy World doth wear,

    How unconcern'd am I ?

I cannot fear to tumble lower

    That never could be high.

Secure in theſe unenvi'd walls

    I think not on the State,

And pity no mans caſe that falls

    From his Ambition's height.

Silence and Innocence are ſafe ;

    A heart that's nobly true

At all thefe little Arts can laugh

That do the World fubdue.

While others Revel it in State,

Here I'le contented fit,

And think I have as good a Fate

As Wealth and Pomp admit.

Let fome in Courtfhip take delight,

And to th' *Exchange* refort ;

There Revel out a Winter's night,

Not making Love, but Sport.

Thefe never knew a noble Flame,

'Tis Luft, Scorn, or Defign :

While Vanity playes all their Game,

Let Peace and Honour mine.

When the inviting Spring appears,

To *Hide-Parke* let them go,

And hafting thence be full of fears

To lofe *Spring-Garden* fhew.

A

Let others (nobler) feek to gain

   In Knowledge happy Fate,

And others bufie them in vain

   To ftudy wayes of State,

But I, refolved from within,

   Confirmed from without,

In Privacy intend to fpin

   My future Minutes out,

And from this Hermitage of mine

   I banifh all wild toyes,

And nothing that is not Divine

   Shall dare to tempt my Joyes;

There are below but two things good,

   Friendfhip and Honefty,

And only thofe alone I would

   Ask for Felicity,

In this retir'd Integrity,

   Free from both War and noife,

I live not by Necessity,

But wholly by my Choice.

LXII.
To Mrs. Wogan, *my Honoured Friend, on the Death of her Husband.*

DRy up your tears, there's enough shed by you,

And we must pay our share of Sorrows too.

It is no private loss when such men fall,

The World's concern'd, and Grief is general.

But though of our Misfortune we complain,

To him it is injurious and vain.

For since we know his rich Integrity,

His real Sweetness, and full Harmony;

How free his heart and house were to his Friends,

Whom he oblig'd without Design or Ends;

How universal was his Courtesie,

How clear a Soul, how even, and how high;

How

How much he scorn'd disguise or meaner Arts,

But with a native Honour conquer'd Hearts ;

We must conclude he was a Treasure lent,

Soon weary of this sordid Tenement.

The Age and World deserv'd him not, and he

Was kindly snatch'd from future Misery.

We can scarce say he's Dead, but gone to rest,

And left a Monument in ev'ry breast.

For you to grieve then in this sad excess,

Is not to speak your Love, but make it less.

A noble Soul no Friendship will admit,

But what's Eternal and Divine as it.

The Soul is hid in mortal flesh we know,

And all its weaknesses must undergo,

Till by degrees it does shine forth at length,

And gathers Beauty, Purity, and Strength :

But never yet doth this Immortal Ray

Put on full splendour till it put off Day.

So

So Infant Love is in the worthiest breast,

By Sense and Passion fetter'd and opprest;

But by degrees it grows still more refin'd,

And scorning clogs only concerns the Mind,

Now as the Soul you lov'd is here set free

From its material gross capacity;

Your Love should follow him now he is gone,

And quitting Passion, put Perfection on.

Such Love as this will its own good deny,

If its dear Object have Felicity,

And since we cannot his great Loss Reprieve,

Let's not lose you in whom he still doth Live,

For while you are by Grief secluded thus,

It doth appear your Funeral to us.

LXIII. *In*

LXIII.

In memory of the most justly honoured,
Mrs. Owen *of* Orielton.

AS when the ancient World by Reason liv'd,

The *Asian* Monarchs deaths were never griev'd;

Their glorious Lives made all their Subjects call

Their Rites a Triumph, not a Funeral:

So still the Good are Princes, and their Fate

Invites us not to weep, but imitate.

Nature intends a progress of each stage

Whereby weak Man creeps to succeeding Age,

Ripens him for that Change for which he's made,

Where th' active Soul is in her Centre laid.

And since none stript of Infancy complain,

'Cause 'tis both their necessity and gain:

So Age and Death by slow approches come,

And by that just inevitable doom

By

By which the Soul (her cloggy drofs once gone)

Puts on Perfection, and refumes her own.

Since then we mourn a happy Soul, O why

Difturb we her with erring Piety?

Who's fo enamour'd on the beauteous Ground,

When with rich Autumn's livery hung round,

As to deny a Sickle to his Grain,

And not undrefs the teeming Earth again?

Fruits grow for ufe, Mankind is born to die;

And both Fates have the fame necefsity.

Then grieve no more, fad Relatives, but learn;

Sigh not, but profit by your juft concern.

Reade over her Life's volume : wife and good,

Not 'caufe fhe muft be fo, but 'caufe fhe wou'd.

To chofen Vertue ftill a conftant friend,

She faw the Times which chang'd, but did not mend.

And as fome are fo civil to the Sun,

They'd fix his beams, and make the Earth to run:

So

So she unmov'd beheld the angry Fate
Which tore a Church, and overthrew a State:
Still durst be Good, and own the noble Truth,
To crown her Age which had adorn'd her Youth.
Great without Pride, a Soul which still could be
Humble and high, full of calm Majesty.
She kept true state within, and could not buy
Her Satisfaction with her Charity.
Fortune or Birth ne're rais'd her Mind, which stood
Not on her being rich, but doing good.
Oblig'd the World, but yet would scorn to be
Paid with Requitals, Thanks or Vanity.
How oft did she what all the World adore,
Make the Poor happy with her useful store?
So general was her Bounty, that she gave
Equality to all before the Grave.
By several means she different persons ty'd,
Who by her Goodness onely were ally'd.

Her

Her Vertue was her Temper, not her Fit ;

Fear'd nothing but the Crimes which some commit

Scorn'd those dark Arts wch pass for Wisdom now,

Nor to a mean ignoble thing could bow.

And her vast Prudence had no other end,

But to forgive a Foe, endear a Friend :

To use, but slight, the World ; and fixt above,

Shine down in beams of Piety and Love.

Why should we then by poor and just complaint

Prove envious Sinners 'cause she is a Saint ?

Close then the Monument ; let not a Tear

That may prophane her Ashes now appear :

For her best Obsequies are that we be

Prudent and Good, Noble and Sweet, as she.

LXIV. A

LXIV.
A Friend.

1.

LOve, Nature's Plot, this great Creation's Soul,
   The Being and the Harmony of things,
Doth still preserve and propagate the whole,
   From whence Mans Happiness & Safety springs:
The earliest, whitest, blessedst Times did draw
From her alone their universal Law.

2.

Friendship's an Abstract of this noble Flame,
   'Tis Love refin'd and purg'd from all its dross,
The next to Angels Love, if not the same,
   As strong in passion is, though not so gross:
It antedates a glad Eternity,
And is an Heaven in Epitome.

Nobler

3.

Nobler then Kindred or then Marriage-band,
   Becaufe more free ; Wedlock-felicity
It felf doth onely by this Union ftand,
   And turns to Friendfhip or to Mifery.
Force or Defign Matches to pafs may bring,
But Friendfhip doth from Love and Honour fpring.

4.

If Souls no Sexes have, for Men t' exclude
   Women from Friendfhip's vaft capacity,
Is a Defign injurious or rude,
   Onely maintain'd by partial tyranny.
Love is allow'd to us and Innocence,
And nobleft Friendfhips do proceed from thence.

5.

The chiefeft thing in Friends is Sympathy :
   There is a Secret that doth Friendfhip guide,
Which

Which makes two Souls before they know agree,
Who by a thoufand mixtures are ally'd,
And chang'd and loft, fo that it is not known
Within which breaft doth now refide their own.

6.

Effential Honour muft be in a Friend,
   Not fuch as every breath fans to and fro ;
But born within, is its own judge and end,
   And dares not fin though fure that none fhould (know,
Where Friendfhip's fpoke, Honefty's underftood ;
For none can be a Friend that is not Good.

7.

Friendfhip doth carry more then common truft,
   And Treachery is here the greateft fin.
Secrets depofed then none ever muft
   Prefume to open, but who put them in.
They that in one Cheft lay up all their ftock,
Had need be fure that none can pick the Lock.

                                        A Breaft

8.

A breaſt too open Friendſhip does not love;
  For that the others Truſt will not conceal;
Nor one too much reſerv'd can it approve;
  Its own Condition this will not reveal.
We empty Paſsions for a double end;
To be refreſh'd and guarded by a Friend.

9.

Wiſdom and Knowledge Friendſhip does require;
  The firſt for Counſel, this for Company;
And though not mainly, yet we may deſire
  For complaiſance and Ingenuity.
Though ev'ry thing may love, yet 'tis a Rule,
He cannot be a Friend that is a Fool.

10.

Diſcretion uſes Parts, and beſt knows how;
  And Patience will all Qualities commend:

That

That serves a need best, but this doth allow
The Weaknesses and Passions of a Friend.
We are not yet come to the Quire above :
Who cannot Pardon here, can never Love.

11.

Thick Waters shew no Images of things ;
Friends are each others Mirrours, and should be
Clearer then Crystal or the Mountain Springs,
And free from Clouds, Design or Flattery.
For vulgar Souls no part of Friendship share :
Poets and Friends are born to what they are.

12.

Friends should observe & chide each others Faults,
To be severe then is most just and kind;
(thoughts :
Nothing can 'scape their search who know the
This they should give and take with equal Mind.
For Friendship, when this Freedom is deny'd,
Is like a Painter when his hands are ty'd.

O A Friend

13.

A Friend ſhould find out each Neceſſity,

   And then unask'd reliev't at any rate:

It is not Friendſhip, but Formality,

   To be deſir'd ; for Kindneſs keeps no ſtate.

Of Friends he doth the Benefactour prove,

That gives his Friend a means t' expreſs his Love.

14.

Abſence doth not from Friendſhip's right excuſe :

   They who preſerve each others heart and fame

Parting can ne're divide, it may diffuſe ;

   As Liquors which aſunder are the ſame.

Though Preſence help'd them at the firſt to greet,

Their Souls know now without thoſe aids to meet.

15.

Conſtant and Solid, whom no ſtorms can ſhake,

   Nor death unfix, a right Friend ought to be;

                     And

And if condemned to survive, doth make

  No second choice, but Grief and Memory.

But Friendship's best Fate is, when it can spend

  A Life, a Fortune, all to serve a Friend.

LXV.
L'Accord du Bien.

1.

ORder, by which all things are made,

  And this great World's foundation laid,

Is nothing else but Harmony,

Where different parts are brought t'agree.

2.

As Empires are still best maintain'd

By those ways which first their Greatness gain'd :

So in this universal Frame

That made and keeps it is the same.

Thus

3.

Thus all things unto peace do tend;
Even Difcords have it for their end.
The caufe why Elements do fight,
Is but their Inftinct to Unite.

4.

Mufick could never pleafe the Senfe
But by United excellence :
The fweeteft Note which Numbers know,
If ftruck alone, would tedious grow.

5.

Man, the whole World's Epitome,
Is by creation Harmony.
'Twas Sin firft quarrel'd in his breaft,
Then made him angry with the reft.

6.

But Goodnefs keeps that Unity,
And loves its own fociety

So well, that feldom it is known
One real Worth to dwell alone.

7.

And hence it is we Friendfhip call
Not by one Vertue's name, but all.
Nor is it when bad things agree
Thought Union, but Confpiracy.

8.

Nature and Grace, fuch enemies
That when one fell t'other did rife,
Are now by Mercy even-fet,
As Stars in Conftellations met.

9.

f Nature were it felf a fin,
Her Author (God) had guilty been :
But Man by fin contracting ftain,
hall purg'd from that be clear again

10.

To prove that Nature's excellent,
Even Sin it self 's an argument :
Therefore we Nature's stain deplore,
Because it self was pure before.

11.

And Grace destroys not, but refines,
Unveils our Reason, then it shines ;
Restores what was deprest by sin,
The fainting beam of God within.

12.

The main spring (Judgment) rectify'd,
Will all the lesser Motions guide,
To spend our Labour, Love and Care,
Not as things seem, but as they are.

13.

'Tis Fancy lost, Wit thrown away,
In trifles to imploy that Ray,

Which then doth in full luſtre ſhine
When both Ingenuous and Divine.

14.

To Eyes by Humours vitiated
All things ſeem falſly coloured :
So 'tis our prejudicial thought
That makes clear Objects ſeem in fault.

15.

They ſcarce believe united good,
By them 'twas never underſtood :
They think one Grace enough for one,
And 'tis becauſe their ſelves have none.

16.

We hunt Extremes, and run ſo faſt,
We can no ſteddy judgment caſt :
He beſt ſurveys the Circuit round
Who ſtands i'th' middle of the ground.

17.

That happy mean would let us fee
Knowledge and Meeknefs may agree;
And find, when each thing hath its name,
Pafsion and Zele are not the fame.

18.

Who ftudies God doth upwards fly,
And height's ftill leffer to our eye;
And he that knows God, foon will fee
Vaft caufe for his Humility.

19.

For by that fearch it will be known
There's nothing but our Will our own:
And whofo doth that ftcck imploy,
Will find more caufe for Shame then Joy.

20.

We know fo little and fo dark,
And fo extinguifh our own fpark,

That he who furtheſt here can go,
Knows nothing as he ought to know.

21.

It will with the moſt Learned ſute
More to enquire then diſpute :
But Vapours ſwell within a Cloud,
And Ignorance 'tis makes us proud.

22.

So whom their own vain Heart belies,
Like Inflammations quickly riſe :
But that Soul which is truly great
Is loweſt in its own conceit.

23.

Yet while we hug our own miſtake,
We Cenſures, but not Judgments, make;
And thence it is we cannot ſee
Obedience ſtand with Liberty.

24.

Providence still keeps even state ;
But he can best command his Fate,
Whose Art by adding his own Voice
Makes his Necessity his Choice,

25.

Rightly to rule ones self must be
The hardest, largest Monarchy :
Whose Passions are his Master's grown,
Will be a Captive in a Throne.

26.

He most the inward freedom gains,
Who just Submissions entertains :
For while in that his Reason sways,
It is himself that he obeys.

27.

But onely in Eternity
We can these beauteous Unions see ;

For Heaven's self and Glory is
But one harmonious constant Bliss.

LXVI.
Invitation to the Country.

BE kind, my dear *Rosania*, though 'tis true
    Thy Friendship will become thy Penance too ;
Though there be nothing can reward the pain,
Nothing to satisfie or entertain ;
Though all be empty, wild, and like to me,
Who make new Troubles in my Company :
Yet is the action more obliging great ;
'Tis Hardship only makes Desert complete.
But yet to prove Mixtures all things compound,
There may in this be some advantage found ;
For a Retirement from the noise of Towns,
Is that for which some Kings have left their Crowns.

                     And

And Conquerours, whofe Laurel preft the brow,

Have chang'd it for the quiet Myrtle-bow.

For Titles, Honours, and the World's Addrefs,

Are things too cheap to make up Happinefs;

The eafie Tribute of a giddy race,

And pay'd lefs to the Perfon then the place.

So falfe reflected and fo fhort content

Is that which Fortune and Opinion lent,

That who moft try'd it have of it complain'd,

With Titles burthen'd and to Greatnefs chain'd.

For they alone enjoy'd what they poffeft,

Who relifht moft and underftood it beft.

And yet that underftanding made them know

The empty fwift difpatch of all below.

So that what moft can outward things endear,

Is the beft means to make them difappear:

And even that Tyrant (Senfe) doth thefe deftroy,

As more officious to our Grief then Joy.

Thus

hus all the glittering World is but a cheat,

btruding on our Senfe things Grofs for Great.

ut he that can enquire and undifguife,

Vill foon perceive the thing that hidden lies ;

nd find no Joys merit efteem but thofe

hofe Scene lies only at our own difpofe.

an unconcern'd without himfelf may be

is own both Profpect and Security.

ngs may be Slaves by their own Pafsions hurl'd,

it who commands himfelf commands the World.

Country-life afsifts this ftudy beft,

here no diftractions do the Soul arreft :

here Heav'n and Earth lie open to our view,

here we fearch Nature and its Author too ;

ffeft with Freedom and a real State

ook down on Vice, and Vanity, and Fate.

here (my *Rofannia*) will we, mingling Souls,

ty the Folly which the World controuls ;

And

And all thofe *Grandeurs* which the World do prize
We either can enjoy, or can defpife.

LXVII.
In Memory of Mrs. E. H.

AS fome choice Plant cherifh'd by Sun and Air,
   And ready to requite the Gard'ner's care,
Bloffoms and flourifhes, but then we find
Is made the Triumph of fome ruder Wind :
So thy untimely Grave did both entomb
Thy Sweetnefs now, and wonders yet to come,
Hung full of hopes thou felt'ft a lovely prize,
Juft as thou didft attract all Hearts and Eyes.
Thus we might apprehend, for had thy years
Been lengthen'd to have pay'd thofe vaft arrears
The World expected, we fhould then conclude,
The Age of Miracles had been renew'd.

For

For thou already haſt with eaſe found out

What others ſtudy with ſuch pains and doubt ;

That frame of Soul which is content alone,

And needs no Entertainment but its own.

Thy even Mind, which made thee good and great,

Was to thee both a ſhelter and retreat.

Of all the Tumults which the World do fill

Thou wert an unconcern'd Spectatour ſtill :

And, were thy duty punctually ſupply'd,

Indifferent to all the World beſide.

Thou wert made up with a Reſolv'd and fix'd,

And wouldſt not with a baſe Allay be mix'd ;

Above the World, couldſt equally deſpiſe

Both its Temptations and its Injuries ;

Couldſt ſumme up all, and find not worth deſire

Thoſe glittering Trifles which the moſt admire ;

But with a nobler aim, and nobler born,

Look down on Greatneſs with contempt and ſcorn.

Thou

Thou hadſt no Arts that others this might ſee,
Nor lov'dſt a Trumpet to thy Piety :
But ſilent and retir'd, calm and ſerene,
Stol'ſt to thy bleſsed Haven hardly ſeen.
It were vain to deſcribe thee then, but now
Thy vaſt acceſsion harder is to know ;
How full of light, and ſatiſfy'd thou art,
So early from this treach'rous World to part ;
How pleas'd thou art reflexions now to make,
And find thou didſt not things below miſtake ;
In how abſtracted converſe thou doſt live,
How much thy Knowledge is intuitive ;
How great and bright a glory is enjoy'd
With Angels, and in Myſteries employ'd.
,Tis ſin then to lament thy Fate, but we
Should help thee to a new Eternity ;
And by ſucceſsive Imitation ſtrive,
Till Time ſhall die, to keep thee ſtill alive ;

And

nd (by thy great Example furnish'd) be
lore apt to live then write this Elogy.

LXVIII.
Submiſſion.

Tis ſo, and humbly I my will reſign,
   Nor dare diſpute with Providence Divine;
t vain, alas! we ſtruggle with our chains,
ut more entangled by the fruitleſs pains.
or as i'th' great Creation of this All
lothing by chance could in ſuch order fall,
.nd what would ſingle be deform'd confeſt,
;rows beauteous in its union with the reſt:
o Providence like Wiſdom we allow,
For what created once does govern now)
.nd the ſame Fate that ſeems to one Reverſe,
; neceſſary to the Univerſe.

               P   **Aii**

All these particular and various things,

Link'd to their Causes by such secret Springs,

Are held so fast, and govern'd by such Art,

That nothing can out of its order start.

The World's God's watch, where nothing is so smal,

But makes a part of what composes all:

Could the least Pin be lost or else displac'd,

The World would be disorder'd and defac'd.

It beats no Pulse in vain, but keeps its time,

And undiscern'd to its own height doth climb;

Strung first, and daily wound up by his hand

Who can its motions guide or understand.

No secret cunning then nor multitude

Can Providence divert, cross or delude.

And her just full decrees are hidden things,

Which harder are to find then Births of Springs,

Yet all in various Consorts fitly found,

And by their Discords Harmony compound.

Hence

Hence is that Order, Life and Energy,

Whereby Forms are preferv'd though Matters die;

And fhifting drefs keep their own living feat :

So that what kills this, does that propagate.

This made the ancient Sage in Rapture cry,

That fure the World had full Eternity.

For though it felf to Time and Fate fubmit,

He's above both who made and governs it;

And to each Creature hath fuch Portion lent,

As Love and Wifdom fees convenient.

For he's no Tyrant, nor delights to grieve

The Beings which from him alone can live.

He's moft concern'd, and hath the greateft fhare

In man, and therefore takes the greateft care

To make him happy, who alone can be

So by Submifsion and Conformity.

For why fhould Changes here below furprize,

When the whole World its refolution tries?

Where

Where were our Springs, our Harvests pleasant use,

Unless Vicissitude did them produce ?

Nay, what can be so wearisome a pain

As when no Alterations entertain ?

To lose, to suffer, to be sick and die,

Arrest us by the same Necessity.

Nor could they trouble us, but that our mind

Hath its own glory unto dross confin'd.

For outward things remove not from their place ,

Till our Souls run to beg their mean embrace;

Then doating on the choice make it our own,

By placing Trifles in th' Opinion's Throne.

So when they are divorc'd by some new cross,

Our Souls seem widow'd by the fatal loss :

But could we keep our Grandeur and our state,

Nothing below would seem unfortunate;

But Grace and Reason, which best succours bring ,

Would with advantage manage every thing ;

And

nd by right Judgment would prevent our moan

or lofing that which never was our own.

or right Opinion's like a Marble grott,

i Summer cool, and in the Winter hot;

Principle which in each Fortune lives,

eftowing Catholick Prefervatives.

is this refolves, there are no loffes where

ertue and Reafon are continued there.

he meaneft Soul might fuch a Fortune fhare,

it no mean Soul could fo that Fortune bear.

hus I compofe my thoughts grown infolent,

s th' *Irifh* harper doth his Inftrument;

hich if once ftruck doth murmure and complain,

it the next touch will filence all again.

P 3   LXIX.

LXIX.

2 Cor. 5. 19. God was in Chriſt Reconciling the World to himſelf.

WHen God, contracted to Humanity,
   Could ſigh and ſuffer, could be ſick and die;
When all the heap of Miracles combin'd
To form the greateſt, which was, ſave Mankind:
Then God took ſtand in Chriſt, ſtudying a way
How to repair the R uin'd World's decay.
His Love, Pow'r, Wiſdom, muſt ſome means procure
His Mercy to advance, Juſtice ſecure:
And ſince Man in ſuch Miſery was hurl'd,
It coſt him more to ſave then made the World.
Oh! what a deſp'rate load of ſins had we,
When God muſt plot for our Felicity:
When God muſt beg us that he may forgive,
And dy himſelf before Mankind could live:

                   And

And what still are we, when our King in vain
begs his lost Rebels to be Friends again ?
What flouds of Love proceed from Heaven's smile,
at once to pardon and to reconcile?
Oh wretched Men! who dare your God confine,
like those who separate what he does joyn.
To stop the Rivers with an Infant's hand,
or count with your Arithmetick the Sand ;
Forbid the Light, the fertile Earth perswade
to shut her bosome from the Lab'rer's Spade :
And yield your God (if these cannot be done)
as universal as the Sea or Sun.
That God hath made he therefore cannot hate,
For 'tis one act to Love and to Create :
And he's too perfect full of Majesty,
to need additions from our Misery.
He hath a Father's, not a Tyrant's, joy ;
'Tis equal Pow'r to save, as to destroy.

Did there ten thousand Worlds to ruine fall,

One God could save, one Christ redeem them all.

Be silent then, ye narrow Souls, take heed

Lest you restrain the Mercy you will need.

But, O my Soul, from these be different,

Imitate thou a nobler Precedent :

As God with open Arms the World does woe,

Learn thou like God to be enlarged too ;

As he begs thy consent to pardon thee,

Learn to submit unto thy Enemy;

As he stands ready thee to entertain,

Be thou as forward to return again;

As he was Crucify'd for and by thee,

Crucifie thou what caus'd his Agony ;

And like to him be mortify'd to sin,

Die to the World as he dy'd for it then.

LXX. *The*

L X X.
The World.

WE falfly think it due unto our Friends,
    That we fhould grieve for their untimely
e that furveys the World with ferious eyes, (ends.
nd ftrips her from her grofs and weak difguife,
hall find 'tis Injury to mourn their Fate ;
e onely dies untimely who dies late.
or if 'twere told to Children in the Womb,
o what a Stage of Mifchiefs they muft come ;
ould they forefee with how much toil and fweat
Men court that guilded nothing, being Great ;
What pains they take not to be what they feem,
Rating their blifs by others falfe efteem ,
And facrificing their Content, to be
Guilty of grave and ferious Vanity ;

How

How each Condition hath its proper Thorns,

And what one man admires, another scorns ;

How frequently their Happiness they miss,

And so far from agreeing what it is,

That the same Person we can hardly find

Who is an hour together in one mind :

Sure they would beg a Period of their breath,

And what we call their Birth would count their
(Death.

Mankind are mad ; for none can live alone,

Because their Joys stand by comparison :

And yet they quarrel at Society,

And strive to kill they know not whom, nor why,

We all live by Mistake, delight in Dreams,

Lost to our selves, and dwelling in Extremes ;

Rejecting what we have, though ne're so good,

And prizing what we never understood.

Compar'd t'our boisterous inconstancy

Tempests are calm, and Discords harmony.

Hence

Hence we reverfe the World, and yet do find

The God that made can hardly pleafe our Mind.

We live by chance, and flip into Events;

Have all of Beafts except their Innocence.

The Soul, which no man's pow'r can reach, a thing

That makes each Woman Man, each Man a King,

Doth fo much lofe, and from its height fo fall,

That fome contend to have no Soul at all.

I is either not obferv'd, or at the beft

By Pafsion fought withall, by Sin depreft.

Freedom of Will (God's Image) is forgot;

And, if we know it, we improve it not.

Our Thoughts, though nothing can be more our

Are ftill unguided, very feldom known. (own,

Time 'fcapes our hands as Water in a Sieve,

We come to die e're we begin to live.

Truth, the moft futable and noble prize,

Food of our Spirits, yet neglected lies.

Errour

Errour and Shadows are our choice, and we
Owe our perdition to our own decree.
If we search Truth, we make it more obscure ;
And when it shines, we can't the light endure.
For most men now, who plod, and eat, and drink,
Have nothing less their bus'ness then to think.
And those few that enquire, how small a share
Of Truth they find, how dark their Notions are !
That serious Evenness that calms the Breast,
And in a Tempest can bestow a Rest,
We either not attempt, or else decline,
By ev'ry trifle snatch'd from our design.
(Others he must in his deceits involve,
Who is not true unto his own Resolve.)
We govern not our selves, but loose the Reins,
Courting our Bondage to a thousand chains ;
And with as many Slaveries content
As there are Tyrants ready to torment,

　　　　　　　　　　　　　　We

We live upon a Rack extended ſtill
To one Extreme or both, but always ill.
For ſince our Fortune is not underſtood,
We ſuffer leſs from bad then from the good.
The Sting is better dreſt and longer laſts,
As Surfeits are more dangerous then Faſts.
And to complete the miſery to us,
We ſee Extremes are ſtill contiguous.
And as we run ſo faſt from what we hate,
Like Squibs on Ropes, to know no middle ſtate ;
To outward ſtorms ſtrengthned by us, we find
Our Fortune as diſordered as our Mind.
But that's excus'd by this, it doth its part ;
A trech'rous World befits a trech'rous Heart.
All ill's our own, the outward ſtorms we lothe
Receive from us their Birth, their Sting, or both.
And that our Vanity be paſt a doubt,
Tis one new Vanity to find it out.

Happy

Happy are they to whom God gives a Grave,

And from themfelves as from his wrath doth fave:

'Tis good not to be born ; but if we muft,

The next good is, foon to return to duft.

When th' uncag'd Soul fled to Eternity

Shall reft, and live, and fing, and love, and fee.

Here we but crawl and grapple, play and cry ;

Are firft our own, then others, enemy :

But there fhall be defac'd both ftain and fcore,

For Time, and Death, and Sin fhall be no more.

L X X I.
The Soul.

1.

HOw vain a thing is Man, whofe nobleft part,

 That Soul wch through the World doth come,

Traverfes Heav'n, finds out the depths of Art,

 Yet is fo ignorant at home:

In

2.

In every Brook our Mirrour we can find
   Reflections of our face to be ;
But a true Optick to prefent our Mind
   We hardly get, and darkly fee.

3.

Yet in the fearch after our felves we run,
   Actions and Caufes we furvey ;
And when the weary Chafe is almoft done,
   Then from our Queft we flip away.

4.

'Tis ftrange and fad, that fince we do believe
   We have a Soul muft never die,
There are fo few that can a Reafon give
   How it obtains that Life, or why.

5.

I wonder not to find thofe that know moft,
   Profefs fo much their Ignorance ;

Since

Since in their own Souls greateſt Wits are loſt,
　　And of themſelves have ſcarce a glance.

6.

But ſomewhat ſure doth here obſcurely lie,
　　That above Droſs would fain advance,
And pants and catches at Eternity,
　　As 'twere its own Inheritance.

7.

A Soul ſelf-mov'd, which can dilate, contract,
　　Pierces and judges things unſeen :
But this groſs heap of Matter cannot act,
　　Unleſs impulſed from within.

8.

Diſtance and Quantity, to Bodies due,
　　The ſtate of Souls cannot admit ;
And all the Contraries which Nature knew
　　Meet there, nor hurt themſelves nor it.

God

9.

God never made a Body so bright and clean,
    Which Good and Evil could discern :
What these words Honesty and Honour mean,
    The Soul alone knows how to learn.

10.

Aud though 'tis true she is imprison'd here,
    Yet hath she Notions of her own,
Which Sense doth onely jog, awake, and clear,
    But cannot at the first make known.

11.

The Soul her own felicity hath laid,
    And independent on the Sense
Sees the weak terrours which the World invade
    With pity or with negligence.

12.

So unconcern'd she lives, so much above
    The Rubbish of a clotty Jail,

That

POEMS.

That nothing doth her Energy improve
So much as when thofe ftructures fail;

13.

She's then a fubftance fubtile, ftrong and pure,
So immaterial and refin'd,
As fpeaks her from the Body's fate fecure,
As wholly of a diff'rent kind.

14.

Religion for reward in vain would look,
Vertue were doom'd to mifery,
All actions were like bubbles in a brook,
Were it not for Mortality.

15.

And as that Conquerour who Millions fpent
Thought it too mean to give a Mite;
So the World's Judge can never be content
To beftow lefs then Infinite.

Treafo

16,

Treason againſt Eternal Majeſty
   Muſt have eternal Juſtice too ;
And ſince unbounded Love did ſatisfie,
   He will unbounded Mercy ſhew.

17.

It is our narrow thoughts ſhorten theſe things,
   By their companion Fleſh inclin'd ;
Which feeling its own weakneſs gladly brings
   The ſame opinion to the Mind.

18,

We ſtifle our own Sun, and live in Shade ;
   But where its beams do once appear,
They make that perſon of himſelf afraid,
   And to his own acts moſt ſevere.

19,

For ways to ſin cloſe, and our breaſts diſguiſe
   From outward ſearch, we ſoon may find :

But

But who can his own Soul bribe or surprise,
  Or sin without a sting behind ?

20.

He that commands himself is more a Prince
  Then he who Nations keeps in aw ;
And those who yield to what their Souls convince,
  Shall never need another Law.

LXXII.
Happiness.

NAture courts Happiness, although it be
  Unknown as the *Athenian* Deity.
It dwells not in Man's Sense, yet he supplies
That want by growing fond of its disguise.
The false appearances of Joy deceive,
And seeking her unto her like we cleave.
For sinning Man hath scarce sense left to know
Whether the Plank he grasps will hold or no.

                                    While

While all the bufinefs of the World is this,

To feek that Good which by miftake they mifs,

And all the feveral Pafsions men exprefs

Are but for Pleafure in a diff'rent drefs,

They hope for Happinefs in being Great,

Or Rich, or Lov'd, then hug their own conceit,

And thofe which promife what they never had,

I'th' midft of Laughter leave the fpirit fad,

But the Good man can find this treafure out,

For which in vain others do dig and doubt;

And hath fuch fecret full Content within,

Though all abroad be ftorms, yet he can fing,

His peace is made, all's quiet in that place,

Where Nature's cur'd and exercis'd by Grace.

This inward Calm prevents his Enemies,

For he can neither envy nor defpife:

But in the beauty of his ordered Mind

Doth ftill a new rich fatisfaction find.

Innocent

Innocent Epicure! whose single breast
Can furnish him with a continual feast.
A Prince at home, and Sceptres can refuse;
Valuing onely what he cannot lose.
He studies to doe good; (a man may be
Harmless for want of Opportunity:)
But he's industrious kindness to dispence,
And therein onely covets eminence.
Others do court applause and fame, but he
Thinks all that giddy noise but Vanity.
He takes no pains to be observ'd or seen,
While all his acts are echoed from within.
He's still himself, when Company are gone,
Too well employ'd ever to be alone.
For studying God in all his volumes, he
Begins the business of Eternity.
And unconcern'd without, retains a power
To suck (like Bees) a sweet from ev'ry flower.

And

And as the Manna of the *Ifraelites*

Had feveral taftes to pleafe all Appetites :

So his Contentment is that catholick food,

That makes all ftates feem fit as well as good.

He dares not wifh, nor his own fate propound ;

But, if God fends, reads Love in every wound :

And would not lofe for all the joys of Senfe

The glorious pleafures of Obedience.

His better part can neither change nor lofe,

And all God's will can bear, can doe, can chufe.

LXXIII.
Death.

1.

HOw weak a Star doth rule Mankind,
 Which owes its ruine to the fame
Caufes which Nature had defign'd
 To cherifh and preferve the frame !

2.

As Commonwealths may be fecure,
 And no remote Invafion dread ;
Yet may a fadder fall endure
 From Traitors in their bofom bred ;

3.

So while we feel no violence,
 And on our active Health do truft,
A fecret hand doth fnatch us hence,
 And tumbles us into the duft.

4.

Yet carelefly we run our race,

    As if we could Death's fummons wave ;

And think not on the narrow fpace

    Between a Table and a Grave.

5.

But fince we cannot Death reprieve,

    Our Souls and Fame we ought to mind,

For they our Bodies will furvive ;

    That goes beyond, this ftayes behind.

6.

If I be fure my Soul is fafe,

    And that my Actions will provide

My Tomb a nobler Epitaph,

    Then that I onely liv'd and dy'd,

7.

So that in various accidents

    I Confcience may and Honour keep ;

                       I with

I with that ease and innocence

   Shall die, as Infants go to sleep.

LXXIV.

*To the Queen's Majesty, on her late
Sickness and Recovery.*

THe publick Gladness that's to us restor'd,

   For your escape from what we so deplor'd,

Will want as well resemblance as belief,

Unless our Joy be measur'd by our Grief.

When in your Fever we with terrour saw

At once our Hopes and Happiness withdraw ;

And every *crisis* did with jealous fear

Enquire the News we scarce durst stay to hear.

Some dying Princes have their Servants slain,

That after death they might not want a Train.

Such cruelty were here a needless sin ;

For had our fatal Fears prophetick been,

Sor-

Sorrow alone that service would have done,

And you by Nations had been waited on.

Your danger was in ev'ry Visage seen,

And onely yours was quiet and serene.

But all our zealous Grief had been in vain,

Had not Great *Charles*'s call'd you back again:

Who did your suff'rings with such pain discern,

He lost three Kingdoms once with less concern.

Lab'ring your safety he neglected his,

Nor fear'd he Death in any shape but this.

His *Genius* did the bold Distemper tame,

And his rich Tears quench'd the rebellious Flame.

At once the *Thracian* Hero lov'd and griev'd,

Till he his lost Felicity retriev'd ;

And with the moving accents of his wo

His Spouse recover'd from the shades below.

So the King's grief your threatned loss withstood,

Who mourn'd with the same fortune that he woo'd:

And

And to his happy Paſſion we have been

Now twice oblig'd for ſo ador'd a Queen.

But how ſevere a Choice had you to make,

When you muſt Heav'n delay, or Him forſake?

Yet ſince thoſe joys you made ſuch haſte to find

Had ſcarce been full if he were left behind,

How well did Fate decide your inward ſtrife,

By making him a Preſent of your Life?

Which reſcu'd Bleſsing we muſt long enjoy,

Since our Offences could it not deſtroy.

For none but Death durſt rival him in you;

And Death himſelf was baffled in it too.

F I N I S.

Errata.

For Rofannia *read* Rofania *throughout.*   *Pag.* 8 1. *for* Bodifcift *read* Bodidrift.

LXXV.
Upon Mr. Abraham Cowley's Retirement.

O D E.

I.

NO, no, unfaithful World, thou haft
   Too long my eafie Heart betray'd,
And me too long thy Foot-ball made :
But I am wifer grown at laft,
And will improve by all that I have paft.
I know 'twas juft I fhould be practis'd on ;
   For I was told before,
And told in fober and inftructive lore,
How little all that trufted thee have won :
And yet I would make hafte to be undone.
Now by my fuff'ring I am better taught,
And fhall no more commit that ftupid fault.

R   Go,

Go, get some other Fool,

Whom thou mayst next cajole:

On me thy frowns thou dost in vain bestow;

For I know how

To be as coy and as reserv'd as thou,

2.

In my remote and humble seat

Now I'm again possest

Of that late fugitive, my Breast,

From all thy tumults and from all thy heat

I'le find a quiet and a cool retreat;

And on the Fetters I have worn

Look with experienc'd and revengeful scorn

In this my sov'raign Privacy.

'Tis true I cannot govern thee,

But yet my self I may subdue;

And that's the nobler Empire of the two.

If ev'ry Pafsion had got leave

   Its fatisfaction to receive,

Yet I would it a higher pleafure call,

To conquer one, then to indulge them all.

            3.

   For thy inconftant Sea, no more

   I'le leave that fafe and folid Shore :

   No, though to profper in the cheat,

   Thou fhouldft my Deftiny defeat,

And make me be Belov'd, or Rich, or Great :

   Nor from my felf fhouldft me reclaim

With all the noife and all the pomp of Fame,

   Judicioufly I'le thee defpife ;

Too fmall the Bargain, and too great the Price,

      For them to cozen twice.

   At length this fecret I have learn'd ;

Who will be happy, will be unconcern'd,

Must all their Comfort in their Bosom wear,
And seek their treasure and their power there.

4.

No other Wealth will I aspire,
   But of Nature to admire ;
Nor envy on a Laurel will bestow,
Whil'st I have any in my Garden grow.
     And when I would be Great,
    'Tis but ascending to a Seat
Which Nature in a lofty Rock hath built ;
A Throne as free from trouble as from guilt.
    Where when my Soul her wings does raise
    Above what Worldlings fear or praise,
With innocence and quiet pride I'le sit,
And see the humble Waves pay tribute to my feet.
O Life Divine, when free from joys diseas'd,
Not always merry, but 'tis always pleas'd !

              A Heart,

5.

A Heart, which is too great a thing

To be a Prefent for a *Perfian* King,

Which God himfelf would have to be his Court,

Where Angels would officioufly refort,

    From its own height fhould much decline,

    If this Converfe it fhould refign

        (Ill-natur'd World!) for thine.

Thy unwife rigour hath thy Empire loft ;

    It hath not onely fet me free,

        But it hath made me fee,

They onely can of thy poffefsion boaft,

Who do enjoy thee leaft, and underftand thee moft.

For lo, the Man whom all Mankind admir'd,

(By ev'ry Grace adorn'd, and ev'ry Mufe infpir'd)

    Is now triumphantly retir'd.

The mighty *Cowley* this hath done,
And over thee a *Parthian* Conqueſt won :
Which future Ages ſhall adore,
And which in this ſubdues thee more
Then either *Greek* or *Roman* ever could before

FINIS.

CPSIA information can be obtained at www.ICGtesting.com
Printed in the USA
LVOW131743061011

249424LV00011B/101/P